BONNIE D. **HOUCK**

SANDI **NOVAK**

ASCD

ALEXANDRIA, VIRGINIA USA

LITERACY UNLEASHED

Fostering Excellent Reading Instruction Through Classroom Visits

1703 N. Beauregard St. • Alexandria, VA 22311-1714 USA
Phone: 800-933-2723 or 703-578-9600 • Fax: 703-575-5400
Website: www.ascd.org • E-mail: member@ascd.org
Author guidelines: www.ascd.org/write

Deborah S. Delisle, *Executive Director;* Robert D. Clouse, *Managing Director, Digital Content & Publications;* Stefani Roth, *Publisher;* Genny Ostertag, *Director, Content Acquisitions;* Carol Collins, *Acquisitions Editor;* Julie Houtz, *Director, Book Editing & Production;* Miriam Calderone, *Editor;* Melissa Johnston, *Graphic Designer;* Mike Kalyan, *Manager, Production Services;* Keith Demmons, *Production Designer*

PAPERBACK ISBN: 978-1-4166-2233-8   ASCD product #116042   n7/16

PDF E-BOOK ISBN: 978-1-4166-2235-2; see Books in Print for other formats.

Quantity discounts: 10–49, 10%; 50+, 15%; 1,000+, special discounts (e-mail programteam@ascd.org or call 800-933-2723, ext. 5773, or 703-575-5773). For desk copies, go to www.ascd.org/deskcopy.

Library of Congress Cataloging-in-Publication Data

Names: Houck, Bonnie D., author. | Novak, Sandi, 1953- author.
Title: Literacy unleashed : fostering excellent reading instruction through
   classroom visits / Bonnie D. Houck and Sandi Novak.
Description: Alexandria, Virginia, USA : ASCD, [2016] | Includes
   bibliographical references and index.
Identifiers: LCCN 2016016141 (print) | LCCN 2016024002 (ebook) | ISBN
   9781416622338 (pbk.) | ISBN 9781416622352 (E-BOOK) | ISBN 9781416622352
   (PDF)
Subjects: LCSH: Reading--United States. | Literacy--Study and teaching.
Classification: LCC LB1050 .H668 2016 (print) | LCC LB1050 (ebook) | DDC
   372.4--dc23
LC record available at https://lccn.loc.gov/2016016141

23 22 21 20 19 18 17 16   1 2 3 4 5 6 7 8 9 10 11 12

LITERACY UNLEASHED

Fostering Excellent Reading Instruction Through Classroom Visits

Acknowledgments	vii
INTRODUCTION	1
PART I: DEVELOPING AND LEADING A LITERACY CULTURE	7
1. Making the Case for the Literacy Classroom Visit Model	9
2. The Elements of Effective Literacy Instruction	18
3. Knowing What to Look For: The Basics	29
PART II: PUTTING THE LCV PROCESS INTO ACTION	41
4. Implementing the Literacy Classroom Visit Model	43
5. Data Analysis and Common Patterns	59
6. Planning for Professional Growth	78
7. Whole-School Involvement Across All Content Areas	94
Part III: CREATING A UNIFIED SYSTEM	111
8. Using the Literacy Classroom Visit Model Across a School District	113
CONCLUSION	121
Appendix A: Information About Literacy Classroom Visits	123
Appendix B: Additional Literacy Classroom Visit Forms	141
Appendix C: List of Videos	147
References	149
Index	156
About the Authors	161

Acknowledgments

We developed the content of this book over the course of many years of collaboration with phenomenal educational leaders. We cannot begin to thank all of the committed leaders and wonderful students who inspired us.

Our ASCD Editors

Carol Collins, Senior Acquisitions Editor at ASCD, encouraged and guided our work over the course of a year as we crafted the content of the text. Carol's wisdom and thoughtful questions motivated us to dig deeper and describe the work with concise clarity.

Miriam Calderone, Associate Editor at ASCD, guided our process in refining the structure of the book. Miriam patiently led us through the challenge of choosing the right title, cover design, and other critical details that created a polished final product.

Supporting Organizations and School Districts

The Minnesota Elementary School Principals Association (MESPA)—especially P. Fred Storti, Olivia Gault, and John Millerhagen—support the important work of providing principals and educational leaders with literacy-focused professional learning experiences.

We would like to thank our amazing partner school districts and all of their wonderful educators, including Mounds View Public Schools, Eastern Carver County School District 112, Lakeville Area Schools, and Barnum Public Schools.

Our partner district leaders, principals, and teachers served as boots on the ground as we refined our process. To Dawn Wiegand, Nancy Wittman-Beltz, and the many teachers who opened their classrooms to us for videotaping: we appreciate your willingness to shine a spotlight on teaching and learning.

Last, but certainly not least, our families offered continuous support (and forgiveness) as we spent evenings and weekends working on the book. Michael Houck, you tirelessly read draft after draft, offering your experience as a teacher to ask clarifying questions and your expertise as a proofreader to notice our errors. We thank you!

Introduction

In this book, we aim to provide school leaders and literacy leaders with the essential tools and resources to create a culture of literacy, reflective practice, and continual learning among staff and students. The processes and practices shared in these pages will help you develop a deeper understanding of quality literacy instruction and strengthen your ability to identify and discuss the instruction necessary for ongoing development of student literacy.

Although literacy is an aggregate of many skills, including reading, writing, listening, and speaking, our Literacy Classroom Visit (LCV) Model focuses principally on reading development as the necessary foundation of overall literacy instruction. Accordingly, this book offers a repertoire of literacy tools, classroom observation formats, checklists, and conferencing templates that you can readily use to identify and address needs around literacy teaching and learning in your school or district.

Why Focus on Literacy?

If you are a principal or superintendent, you may be wondering whether learning about ways to evaluate and improve the quality of reading instruction in your school or district is a wise investment of your time. With so many other priorities—curriculum, instruction, staff development, school climate and safety, and family engagement, among others—why put literacy at the top of the list? Read on.

Where We Are

Most of us can probably agree that developing students into accomplished lifelong readers is the cornerstone of learning and educational achievement, providing the means by which students gain most of their content knowledge both in and out of school. But literacy also has long-range benefits that extend beyond the academic sphere. The ability to read not only makes us better learners and communicators but also arms us against oppression and benefits us financially (Gallagher, 2003): witness the strong correlation between literacy difficulties and dropout rates, incarceration, and welfare status. In addition, somewhere between one-half and two-thirds of new jobs in the future will require a college education and higher-level literacy skills (Graham & Hebert, 2010).

Unfortunately, the United States is failing to meet the goal of teaching all students to read. Forty percent of high school graduates lack the required literacy skills that employers desire (National Governors Association Center for Best Practices, 2005), and two-thirds of students at the 4th and 8th grade levels are not proficient readers (National Assessment of Educational Progress, 2014). These data have remained essentially unchanged for more than two decades, despite the heavy emphasis on reading instruction and assessment that's been in place since the implementation of the No Child Left Behind Act of 2001.

Where We Need to Go

Clearly, something needs to change. The Common Core State Standards have made a start by bringing renewed attention to the need for *all* teachers—at every grade level and in every subject area—to be literacy teachers. We can't overstate the importance of this.

Good literacy instruction is essential throughout K–12 education. Preschool through 3rd grade are years of vital development: if children do not reach progressive milestones in these early years, they have little chance of ever catching up (Juel, 1994). The learning doesn't stop after these early grades, though: a student reading proficiently at, say, 5th grade will remain at the same reading level in subsequent grades unless he or she is consistently taught strategies to glean knowledge from more difficult and specialized texts (Joftus, 2002). Although some reading problems in middle and high school may stem from a lack of quality literacy instruction in the elementary grades, the culprit is more likely a lack of instruction in reading complex text throughout the upper grades (Greenleaf & Hinchman, 2009). Simply put, there's no point at which students are "done" learning to read. They need to continually hone their skills to be able to comprehend, internalize, and transfer knowledge from progressively more complex and sophisticated texts. This is crucial preparation for the demands of college, career, and life.

It is equally important to teach literacy across the content areas. The Common Core State Standards for English Language Arts & Literacy in History/Social Studies, Science, and Technical Subjects (National Governors Association Center for Best Practices & the Council of Chief State School Officers, 2010) aim for students in grades 6–12 to be able to independently build knowledge in these disciplines through reading and writing. Literacy and learning within the content areas of science and social studies have become a requirement for adolescent readers to succeed (Kosanovich, Reed, & Miller, 2010). In a shift from traditional standards, the Common Core places increased emphasis on informational text, and none too soon: in some schools, it is common to have classes in which 75–80 percent of students cannot successfully read their textbooks (Carnine & Carnine, 2004).

Teaching students the skills required to make sense of a variety of texts and write for diverse purposes is an ongoing task to which all teachers must deeply commit themselves, because effective instruction—regardless of school location, student demographics, or financial constraints—leads to greater student learning (Hattie, 2008; Marzano, Pickering, & Pollock, 2004). And, in turn, it is school leaders' job to identify the components of effective instruction so that we can provide the resources and training that teachers need to foster the highest possible gains in student achievement (Colvin & Johnson, 2007; Fisher & Adler, 1999).

Enter the Literacy Classroom Visit Model

We've established *why* ensuring effective literacy instruction is such a high priority for school leaders; *how* to do this is another challenge altogether. This is where our Literacy Classroom Visit Model comes in.

The LCV Model is not a gimmicky framework we came up with over the course of a few days; it's the result of years of observation, coaching, training, data gathering, experimentation, and revision. From 2003 to 2008, Bonnie worked as the state reading specialist in the Minnesota Department of Education. A large portion of her responsibilities consisted of identifying the research-based practices behind effective reading instruction. It became apparent to her that knowing these practices by name did not equip school leaders to be able to recognize them during classroom visits, explain how the practices were being implemented in their schools, or identify the professional development that teachers needed in order to learn and implement these practices. Accordingly, Bonnie worked to develop instruments and processes to help leaders identify effective literacy teaching and student learning. These processes yielded concrete, consistent data that supported districts in their important work of developing quality literacy education.

Our paths crossed when Sandi—then an assistant superintendent in a suburban school district—hired Bonnie as a district literacy coordinator. Sandi's expertise as a leader of leaders and cognitive coach and the breadth of her experience at the school and district levels added new dimensions to the processes that Bonnie had developed.

The Literacy Classroom Visit Model is what emerged from our years of collaboration in guiding school and district leaders in making classroom visits and using data to provide teachers with targeted, actionable feedback. Through conference sessions, leadership workshops, seminar courses, and our work with schools and districts across the United States, the Literacy Classroom Visit Model has evolved into a solid system that schools and districts can use to guide effective literacy teaching and lasting improvement.

How This Book Is Organized

Part I of this book describes the attributes of a strong literacy culture, the importance of literacy leadership, and walkthrough observation models. In this section, we introduce the Literacy Classroom Visit Model and its overarching purpose and goals.

In Part II, we describe how to develop a classroom visit schedule, explaining the number of classrooms to visit, how long to spend in each classroom, how to ensure consistency among visiting teams, and how to identify and describe patterns of practice. We outline ways to determine an area of focus, identified either from previous classroom visits or from other school literacy data; provide examples of data collection techniques and a protocol for data collection; show how well-designed and well-facilitated discussions can provide opportunities for staff to reflect on the nature of teaching and learning; and describe how to take your school's instructional practices to the next level of proficiency. Part II also examines ways in which Literacy Classroom Visits can be modified specifically for content-area classrooms. These data add to the overall knowledge of the literacy culture and instructional delivery in a school or district.

Part III explains how to sustain the LCV Model over time and move beyond a school-focused model to a districtwide system of data collection, reflection, analysis, and action.

Each of the three parts of this book begins with a scenario from a school or district using the Literacy Classroom Visit Model and ends with "Reflection to Action" prompts to help you implement the model in your school or district. Quotations and video clips from educators who are using the LCV Model provide deeper context. These companion videos introduce the concepts of the Literacy Classroom Visit Model, extend the content to help you visualize what it looks like in action, and convey how principals, literacy leaders, and district administrators can use the LCV structure in their schools and districts. You can find a list of the videos in Appendix C, and they're available at www.ascd.org/Publications/Books /Literacy-Unleashed-Book-Video-Clips.aspx. We use the icon pictured to the left throughout the book to indicate these videos.

In addition, we have made many of this book's tools and forms available online to fill in or print out. You can access these resources at www.ascd.org/ASCD/pdf/books/houck2016.pdf. Use the password "houck116042" to unlock the PDF.

During the last decade, we have focused on helping teachers and school leaders to integrate high-quality, complex research into the realities of day-to-day teaching. We hold the highest regard for all educators, knowing it is their hard work and passion that have the power to make the greatest difference in our world. We hope our book will support your work and profoundly affect literacy instruction and leadership in your school or district.

PART I:
Developing and Leading a Literacy Culture

SCENARIO: BARNUM ELEMENTARY SCHOOL

Four years ago, teachers at Barnum Elementary School would have told you that their instructional practices were above average—or at least average. However, students' performance on standards-based and achievement assessments during that time told a different story, especially in the area of reading.

With the data challenging our assumptions, we couldn't hide from the reality that we needed to change our teaching practices. We wanted our students to grow and achieve. We did not want the stigma of having underperforming classrooms to cause divisiveness or finger-pointing within our community. By discussing our student data, the leadership team and the teachers decided to come together, create common practices throughout the school, and support both team and individual growth.

We decided to shift the focus from student test scores to our teaching practices. Taking the emphasis off of test scores gave our teachers room to breathe and freed us from the emotional baggage that low test scores can bring, allowing us to grab on to practices that transformed our school's literacy culture.

At first, we purchased resources and tried a variety of "one and done" workshops to broaden our teaching practices. Once we realized that this piecemeal approach was not getting us where we wanted to be, we incorporated the Literacy Classroom Visit Model. The LCV Model provided a way for us to examine our school's literacy culture and the effectiveness of our current instruction. We gained a common language and common expectations. This schoolwide effort didn't happen in a vacuum but was accompanied by plenty of debate, discussion, and professional development.

Over time, we used the LCV Model to gather schoolwide, grade-level, and, eventually, individual teaching data. We moved from having individual and common grade-level practices to setting consistent schoolwide expectations. Our focus on developing a schoolwide culture of literacy helped us provide meaningful professional development tailored to the specific needs of our building, teacher teams, and individual educators. The results speak for themselves: we went from being a Continuous Improvement school where teachers were doing many good things to becoming a Reward School where all teachers are guided by research-supported best practices within our established expectations for literacy.

The LCV Model was instrumental in providing the clarity and focus that we needed across our K–6 instruction. Our test scores and LCV data now prove that we are providing above-average instruction. Just ask any teacher in the building!

Tom Cawcutt, Principal
Barnum Elementary School
Barnum, Minnesota

Making the Case for the Literacy Classroom Visit Model

1

Schools that have successful literacy programs show evidence of strong principal leadership, with focused attention on setting a literacy agenda, supporting teachers, accessing resources, and building a capacity for further growth.

—David Booth and Jennifer Rowsell, *The Literacy Principal*

School leaders assume the heavy responsibility of ensuring continuous learning for both teachers and students. Although many educators who enter the administrative track tend to drift away from the areas of teaching and learning, principals need enough content knowledge to be able to assess the instruction they see (Fink & Resnick, 2001).

The role of the principal as instructional leader is becoming increasingly important in light of the current focus on teacher effectiveness and a growing consensus in the field on what effective teachers do to enhance student learning (MET Project, 2013). Since researchers have begun to quantify the average effects of specific instructional strategies (Marzano et al., 2004), educators should, in theory, be able to close the gap between what they know works and what they are doing in their classrooms.

Yet despite increased scrutiny of literacy instruction, little has been done to examine the specific knowledge that principals need regarding literacy teaching and learning, or how districts can build literacy leadership capacity. As Reeves (2008) noted, "If school leaders really believe that literacy is a priority, then they have a personal responsibility to understand literacy instruction, define it for their colleagues, and observe it daily" (p. 91).

Leaders' Role and the Need for Data

So, how can leaders go about fulfilling this responsibility? Along with the job of recruiting, hiring, and sustaining quality staff who enhance students' overall literacy learning, a literacy leader must gain an understanding of literacy teaching practices and be able to help classroom teachers ensure that all students learn to read, write, and think critically about different kinds of texts. Education leaders who are not proficient in their knowledge of literacy instruction have a difficult time determining the key qualifications that excellent teachers possess (Stein & Nelson, 2003).

Thus, leaders need a system to collect and analyze timely and useful information about (1) the current instructional practices in their schools and (2) how students engage and collaborate in the process of learning. These data must be collected consistently, with a clear purpose and without the intent of using them to evaluate individuals' teaching performance. Data collection should focus on how the instructional learning environment and classroom practices foster student learning, and the data should be used to celebrate areas of success and illuminate areas of need. Leaders can then address the areas of need by providing teachers with targeted professional learning opportunities and other resources. The method of data collection should also provide a way to determine how well these resources and learning experiences are effecting the intended changes in teaching and learning.

The Power of Classroom Visits

Research (Protheroe, 2009) supports the value of regular classroom visits as integral to the ongoing work of education leaders. These visits may take the form of instructional rounds, walkthroughs, observations, or any series of scheduled visits that can either capture broad impressions of overall instruction or home in on key areas. Typically, these visits are done informally for the purpose of data collection and professional growth. However, in some instances, districts and school administrators use them as part of their formal observations in the evaluation process.

Conducting informal observations enables school administrators to evaluate job-embedded professional development initiatives, collect evidence related to curricular programs, and identify trends in instructional practices (Stout, Kachur, & Edwards, 2009). Ideally, the process also provides teachers with the feedback they need to evaluate their own effectiveness in applying their professional learning (Hopkins, 2008).

Frequent, brief ... walkthroughs can foster a school culture of collaborative learning and dialogue. (Ginsberg & Murphy, 2002, p. 34)

Walkthroughs and instructional rounds both have a defined purpose and can provide rich and useful data for education leaders. Establishing time and a process for classroom visits, as these practices do, can help leaders establish themselves as instructional leaders and mentors; familiarize themselves with the climate, curriculum, and practices in the building; and develop partnerships in discussing common practices and needs (Ginsberg & Murphy, 2002). The classroom walkthrough process can also create a framework for designing and evaluating schoolwide professional development (Cervone & Martinez-Miller, 2007) and be used to increase student achievement (Skretta, 2008). Although walkthrough models may vary in design and implementation, their goal remains the same: to enhance student learning and achievement by improving instruction (Scott, 2012). Instructional rounds are another method of gathering data, involving teams that work collaboratively to make sense of their observations and draw logical conclusions (City, Elmore, Fiarman, & Teitel, 2009).

Concerns About Walkthrough Protocols

In practice, classroom observations can fall short of their intended purpose unless considerable care has been given to the walkthrough form and the feedback process. Too often, the walkthrough form consists of broad checklists of generic practices that do not identify a clear purpose or articulate specific instructional "look-fors" and thus do not provide leaders with the information they need to give appropriate or accurate feedback (Pitler & Goodwin, 2008). With respect to literacy in particular, without a clear understanding of what effective literacy instruction looks like, this method accomplishes little (Hoewing, 2011).

Sometimes walkthroughs are used for individual teacher evaluation, which goes against the intent of the original practice. In such cases, feedback is given to individuals after only a few short visits to their classrooms, diminishing trust in the process as well as the leader. As many scholars (DuFour & Marzano, 2009; Liu & Mulfinger, 2011) have asserted, the current teacher evaluation system in many schools across the United States—which incorporates walkthrough practices—is flawed because feedback is infrequent and broad or focused on areas other than quality instruction.

If leaders do not clearly communicate the purpose of their walkthroughs and look for specific, research-supported instructional practices that have been discussed with teachers, the observation and the feedback they provide may be worthless or, worse, damaging to educators and students alike (Pitler & Goodwin, 2008). The process can also create significant anxiety and resistance among teachers. In order to be an effective tool for instructional improvement, the culminating data must be used to identify professional learning and resource needs that are known factors in teacher effectiveness and student achievement (Ginsberg, 2001).

The LCV Model: A Better Way

Literacy Classroom Visits incorporate the best aspects of walkthroughs: they are brief, frequent, informal, and focused visits to classrooms by observers whose purpose is to gather data about teaching practices and engage in collaborative follow-up. Like instructional rounds, Literacy Classroom Visits can be conducted in teams and focus on student learning and collaborative discussion around descriptive, nonjudgmental data. However, they are unique in that they concentrate specifically on research-supported practices that have a direct effect on literacy achievement.

The Literacy Classroom Visit Model is also distinctive in terms of how data are collected and analyzed to direct the focus on specific data patterns. These patterns highlight instruction and learning of the community rather than the practices of individuals. Over time, they reveal evidence of a developing culture of literacy as well as effective practices that integrate balanced literacy instruction and the gradual release of responsibility (approaches that we delve into in subsequent chapters).

No matter how wonderful they are, reading programs, resources, and research-based approaches are productive only when used by effective teachers using proven practices for excellent instruction (Allington, 2002). Finding the sweet spot among what research says about effective instruction, what teachers know and are doing in the classroom, and how these elements intersect with student development can be challenging. The LCV Model provides a solid vehicle to find this crucial intersection, combining research about best practices in literacy instruction and classroom delivery methods with how students engage and learn to read and write. The data gathered during these visits provide the information that teachers need to be most effective.

What Are We Looking For?

Literacy Classroom Visits are seated in research-based practices that are essential to helping students become critical thinkers, effective readers, and meaning makers. The "look-fors" listed on the LCV instrument (see Figure 1.1, also available online; see note on p. 5) are a carefully distilled and field-tested compendium of research-supported instructional practices specific to literacy. In addition, the LCV instrument integrates general instructional best practices, such as the gradual release of responsibility (Pearson & Gallagher, 1983), differentiated instruction (Tomlinson & Allan, 2000), and purposeful student engagement. The resulting formula creates a strong foundation of instructional practices that promote student growth and achievement. **Video 1.1** provides an overview of the full process.

Collecting Literacy Classroom Visit data over time can

- Establish a body of evidence about a school's or district's overall literacy culture and instruction.
- Identify instructional patterns within teacher teams, grade levels, and content areas.
- Pinpoint resource needs and reduce unnecessary budget expenditures.
- Guide planning for professional learning and professional learning community (PLC) team content.
- Establish common beliefs, practices, and language within the community.
- Inform a school community about the implementation of professional learning goals.
- Ensure that students are learning and mastering grade-level standards and expectations.

Figure 1.1 | *Literacy Classroom Visit Instrument*

Teacher/Grade_____ Date/Time _____Observer _____

Classroom Environment and Culture	Notes:
☐ Classroom structure and practices support a developing culture of literacy. ☐ Students are actively and purposefully engaged in literacy-focused learning activities. ☐ Classroom library is organized to support self-selection and class size/level (300+ texts). ☐ Classroom library has a balance of fiction/informational texts at varied levels. ☐ Rituals, routines, and procedures are in place (I-Charts, process for book selection, etc.). ☐ Displays of student work show development and celebrate literacy learning. ☐ Interactive word walls are used to support writing and vocabulary development.	
Learning Target/Instructional Goal	
☐ Learning target/goal is posted in student-friendly language. ☐ Learning target/goal identifies demonstration of learning (performance criteria). ☐ Learning target/goal is taught and monitored across the gradual release of responsibility.	
Observed Method of Instructional Delivery	
☐ Whole-group lesson or mini-lesson ☐ Small-group lesson ☐ Independent reading and application	
Whole-Group Explicit Instruction	
☐ Teacher is leading a focused mini-lesson or lesson using time effectively for age range. ☐ Teacher is explicitly teaching/modeling effective skill/strategy (learning target). ☐ Students are actively listening, purposefully engaged, and interacting with teacher. ☐ Students are actively listening, purposefully engaged, and interacting with peers.	
Small-Group Guided Practice	
☐ Teacher is guiding students' reading, strategy application, and collaborative discussions. ☐ Teacher is listening to students read individually while others read quietly. ☐ Teacher is assessing strengths/needs and collecting anecdotal notes. ☐ Students are reading and discussing texts at their instructional level. ☐ Students are practicing the skill or strategy explicitly taught and modeled in whole group.	

Independent Reading and Application	
☐ Teacher is conferring one-on-one with reader. ☐ Teacher is assessing development and recording data. ☐ Students are reading self-selected books from a bag or bin and applying strategies. ☐ Students are conferring with teacher using skills and demonstrating learning target. ☐ Students are actively working at some other connected literacy enhancement activity.	
Student Interaction and Understanding	
☐ Students can explain the skill/strategy. ☐ Students know what they are supposed to learn and how they are expected to demonstrate that learning in whole or small group or on their own. ☐ N/A (Did not speak with student)	
Comments/Feedback:	
Possible Prompts for Peer Discussions (PLCs):	

Source: © 2014 by Bonnie D. Houck, EdD. Used with permission.

The purpose of any data collection system is to get at the heart of what students are doing and understanding in a holistic way that is quite different from assessment measures (Cervone & Martinez-Miller, 2007). As instructional leaders, principals can systematically work with teachers to learn about what teachers are teaching *and* what students are learning. Literacy Classroom Visits capture and document moments in time that, when woven together, can accurately tell the story of a classroom, grade level, school, or district. This requires not only time and commitment but also an established structure that is supported by trust, continuous learning, and a spirit of inquiry.

The Structure of Literacy Classroom Visits: An Overview

In the chapters to follow, we present a deep examination of what Literacy Classroom Visits look like in practice. For now, here is a brief overview.

Purpose. The predominant purpose of Literacy Classroom Visits is to provide educators with the tools, strategies, and processes to foster learning environments in which students become successful and motivated readers and writers. Through these visits, leaders regularly observe current literacy learning by using an ongoing system of data collection and analysis that informs them of the current literacy practices in their schools or districts.

Literacy Classroom Visits are different from other walkthroughs I have done in the past because I am intentional and my focus is singular in purpose. A classroom is a complicated network of learning experiences and interactions. If a principal tries to observe it all, it can be overwhelming. Literacy Classroom Visits define and outline very specific things to look for, providing more clarity and purpose in why I am visiting the classroom by identifying what data to collect related to improving and meeting the literacy needs of our students.

Abe Rodemeyer, Principal

Process. Literacy Classroom Visits are an ongoing series of short (three- to five-minute), planned visits specifically focused on best practices of literacy instruction and learning. Literacy Classroom Visits occur frequently throughout the course of each school year. They provide multiple firsthand snapshots of teaching and learning that take the pulse of literacy within a school and distinguish patterns in practice that can be used to inform instruction and improvement efforts.

Use of data. Data from a single, brief classroom visit are not useful. In contrast, the data patterns that emerge over time through regular visits provide a rich tapestry of insight into student learning and teacher development. Analyzing the accumulated data requires reflection and conversation about the patterns that arise. These data conversations can take place among leaders or groups of teachers or across a teaching community.

Implementation and ongoing practice. The data from the visits are used not to evaluate teachers but to illuminate what teachers need to support their literacy instruction and ensure student growth. As these needs are identified, leaders reflect on which resources and professional learning opportunities have the greatest effect on teaching and learning. As resources are obtained and new practices are learned, Literacy Classroom Visits can be modified to collect specific data to determine how well the implementation is working. This cyclical process of data collection and review offers valuable formative information that not only supports improvement in instructional delivery but also contributes to high-quality professional development practices.

A Catalyst for Lasting Change

Good leaders recognize the value of effective teachers and the instructional environments they create. Accordingly, they understand how important it is to identify and provide the resources and professional learning experiences that teachers need in order to increase student achievement (DuFour & Mattos, 2013). The LCV Model supports leaders in this essential task by helping them to collect and analyze information about current classroom practices and to provide teachers with the support they need to grow. Used well, the LCV Model is a catalyst for lasting change. By incorporating purposeful Literacy Classroom Visits into their improvement efforts, principals can create—and sustain—a powerful culture of literacy throughout the school community.

The Elements of Effective Literacy Instruction

2

Effective instructional leaders engage in work that supports teachers in improving their instructional practices in classrooms.

—Sally J. Zepeda, *Instructional Supervision*

To develop and maintain effective literacy instruction, both the school and the classroom environment must support a literacy culture. Such a culture is evident as soon as you walk into a school building; you can sense it in the corridors, the main office, and the teachers' lounge (UNESCO, 2011). Such a building abounds with literacy-related displays, resources, and student work. The media center serves as a central hub, offering resources in all content areas. Learners have opportunities to develop and apply their literacy skills through a variety of schoolwide activities (Torres, 2006), and the school's core mission includes goals for literacy. More than its availability of texts and resources, a rich, literate educational environment is defined by its culture of literacy.

But what exactly *is* a literacy culture, and how is it formed? More specifically, what does a classroom with a rich literacy culture look like? The top section of our Literacy Classroom Visit instrument (see Figure 1.1, p. 14) provides a starting point for answering these questions, with its streamlined checklist designed to collect data about the structure of the classroom, the classroom library, the rituals and routines for classroom management, the walls and displays in the classroom, and the type of activities and overall level of student engagement observed. Before we go into these specifics, however, let's examine the twin tenets of effective literacy instruction, upon which all these elements are predicated.

The Twin Tenets of Effective Literacy Instruction

A classroom that supports literacy development fosters a positive and productive culture that incorporates two important, research-based instructional philosophies: balanced literacy and the gradual release of responsibility. These philosophies support each other in providing student-focused instruction that fosters student self-direction, motivation, and achievement.

Balanced Literacy

Balanced literacy instruction (Pressley & Allington, 2014) incorporates explicit, systematic, and direct teaching of literacy skills and strategies; offers frequent opportunities for students to apply those skills and strategies during reading, writing, and discussion of engaging and authentic literature and informational texts; and provides teacher guidance and feedback.

A balanced literacy method of teaching begins with the necessary components of literacy instruction identified by the National Reading Panel (National Institute of Child Health and Human Development, 2000) and the National Early Literacy Panel (2008): oral language development, phonemic awareness, phonics, fluency, vocabulary, and comprehension development. These foundational components are balanced and released through a flow of instruction supported by knowledge about each student's developmental needs.

To achieve this, the teacher identifies learning targets for the class, determines the current level of student development and mastery, and designs instruction to bring students to the next level of learning. Next, the teacher explicitly teaches and models how to meet the learning targets in whole-group or shared sessions. Then he or she turns over the responsibility for the learning to students by differentiating the application and practice of learning targets through structured small-group and independent literacy experiences. The movement across these methods of instructional support and delivery requires continual data collection and differentiation so that the teacher can monitor the progress and development of students as they practice and master literacy skills and strategies.

In a truly balanced literacy program, how you teach is as important as what you teach. (Strickland, 2015, para. 1)

It's important to keep in mind that balanced literacy is a philosophy and a framework for instructional planning and implementation, not a program for teaching reading, writing, or the language arts. It involves the use of observation and assessment to make instructional decisions. That said, this framework has been documented as an effective approach for improving literacy achievement (Taylor, Pressley, & Pearson, 2002). Teachers mentor students into becoming capable thinkers and learners as they develop independent expertise in applying skills and strategies to master goals (Fisher & Frey, 2007).

The Gradual Release of Responsibility

The gradual release of responsibility (Pearson & Gallagher, 1983) has been recognized for more than 30 years as a successful approach to developing a student-centered classroom and self-directed learners. It is sometimes referred to as "I do it, we do it, you do it," because the instructional delivery shifts from demonstration by the teacher to practice and mastery by the student. As new learning is introduced, the teacher plays the prominent role. The gradual release of responsibility moves the ownership of learning from teacher to student over time.

 Video 2.1 provides a glimpse into a 4th grade lesson's gradual release of responsibility from whole group to small group to independent reading, during which students apply the learning target.

To see key attributes that comprise effective literacy teaching and learning written down on a classroom visit form helps me focus my attention and adds clarity to my observations. I believe a model that concentrates on collaborative practice and ways to improve the literacy culture within our school will be more powerful than any other evaluative measure.

Dr. Steven Geis, Princlpal

Combining the Best of Philosophies

To best meet the literacy needs of students, teachers need 90–120 minutes of uninterrupted reading instruction within their 120- to 150-minute language arts block (Taylor, 2007). In many schools, teachers do not have this much time in their schedules for reading-focused instruction. To help teachers streamline their teaching to ensure that they're covering the most important elements of reading instruction, the Foundation for Child Development convened a group of literacy experts. The resulting Minnesota Literacy Think Tank, a group representing a range of expertise in literacy research and instruction, worked together to create the *Balanced Literacy Gradual Release Model of Reading Instruction* (Boehm et al., 2012) (see Figure 2.1, also available online; see note on p. 5).

This document distills the critical components of reading instruction into a concise tool to guide the planning, implementation, and assessment of reading instruction. It is not a comprehensive treatment of every possible instructional strategy a teacher might use but, rather, an outline of what is necessary. It became a key resource for us as we developed the Literacy Classroom Visit Model.

Connections to the Literacy Classroom Visit Model

It can be helpful to know what quality literacy teaching and learning look like before beginning to use the Literacy Classroom Visit instrument, so let's look at the first section of the instrument—Classroom Environment and Culture—filled out with data from an exemplary school (see Figure 2.2). Then we'll examine more closely what qualities the data represent. It is important to take the time to reflect on and develop the literacy culture in your classroom because these elements will support student learning and pave the way to effective instruction. In the following sections, we look at each of these elements in turn.

Classroom Structure

Even if you don't have control over the size of your classroom or its furnishings, you can make some decisions about the flow of the room. A balanced literacy classroom needs an area for whole-group activities, including shared instruction and read-aloud. Bringing students together

Figure 2.1 | *Balanced Literacy Gradual Release Model of Reading Instruction*

Balanced Literacy Gradual Release Model of Reading Instruction (90- to 120-Minute Block)
(Whole group, small group, and independent application may be introduced in short blocks and repeated within the 90–120 minutes.)

Whole-Group Explicit Instruction and Modeling *(10–15–20 minutes—may be repeated)*	Small-Group Guided Practice *(10–20–30 minutes—may be repeated)*	Independent Application and Demonstration of Learning *(15–20–30 minutes—may be repeated)*
Teacher • Selects, reads, and rereads books at or above grade level to expose students to a wide variety of quality texts, language, and rich vocabulary. • Directly explains and explicitly teaches words, concepts, and age-appropriate learning targets and literacy skills and strategies. • Models higher-order thinking, strategic comprehension, and/or word analysis strategies that contribute to students' cognitive processing and knowledge construction. • Thinks aloud to reveal the thought processes and meaning making that effective readers employ while reading.	**Teacher** • Flexibly groups students according to specific learning needs related to the lesson. • Scaffolds instructional tasks so that students are challenged but feel competent and capable of addressing the task with the support of the teacher and other members of the small group. • Coaches and supports small groups of students in reading texts at their instructional level. • Guides students and listens to them read as they apply skills and strategies modeled in whole group. • Specifically discusses key words, concepts, and strategies that support developmental literacy learning. • Engages students in interactive conversations, encouraging participation with peers.	**Teacher** • Develops student stamina to read for 20–30 minutes every day. • Begins with short period (10–15 minutes) and works with students to build resiliency over time. • Develops literacy centers or activities to support student choice while extending literacy skills, strategies, and behaviors that have been taught and modeled but need to be practiced to achieve mastery. • Observes, confers with, and engages in conversation with students regularly to assess their development. • Provides specific, targeted feedback to motivate and develop self-efficacy in students. • Records assessments, observations, and anecdotal notes.

Whole-Group Explicit Instruction and Modeling (10–15–20 minutes—may be repeated)	Small-Group Guided Practice (10–20–30 minutes—may be repeated)	Independent Application and Demonstration of Learning (15–20–30 minutes—may be repeated)
Student • Participates in and actively responds to instruction and learning. • Focuses attention on fiction, nonfiction, skills, strategies, and other forms of instruction. • Asks and answers teacher's questions. • Clarifies learning with partner when prompted by the teacher. • Responds to and participates in the development of written response, sticky notes, graphic organizers, or other tools that foster engagement in the lesson.	**Student** • Actively engages in and practices the learning taught and modeled in whole group, individually, and with peers. • Demonstrates a developing proficiency in reading texts at his or her instructional learning level by applying reading comprehension strategies and skills to make meaning with support of the teacher. • Responds to and generates conversation with a partner and within the small group. • Uses strategies and frameworks such as reciprocal teaching strategies to foster small-group independence.	**Student** • Demonstrates learning objective of core lesson. • Works independently, demonstrating independence in literacy behaviors and applying previously learned strategies taught and modeled in whole group and practiced in small group. • Reads text at his or her developmental, independent, and/or high-interest level. • Practices word work and word analysis strategies. • Writes developmentally appropriate responses to reading. • Works at literacy centers or activities to explore, invent, discover, extend, and problem-solve alone or with peers. • Works with peers in student-led discussion groups, literature circles, book clubs, or projects.

Source: Developed by the Literacy Think Tank (E. Boehm, D. Dillon, L. Helman, B. Houck, G. Jordan, D. Peterson, P. Mogush, B. Murphy). © 2012 by Houck Educational Services. Used with permission. Requests for extended use can be made to HouckReadz@HouckEd.com.

Figure 2.2 | *Classroom Environment and Culture: What It Looks Like*

LCV Look-Fors in a Classroom	Across an Exemplary School
• Classroom structure and practices support a developing culture of literacy. • Students are actively and purposefully engaged in literacy-focused learning activities.	• All classrooms have space for whole- and small-group instruction and independent reading. • Resources are available to support literacy engagement. • All teachers are actively working with students during all aspects of instruction. • All students are engaged in various reading, writing, listening, speaking, and thinking activities.
• Classroom library is organized to support self-selection and class size/level (300+ texts). • Classroom library has a balance of fiction/ informational texts at varied levels.	• All classroom libraries contain a minimum of 300 books. • Classroom libraries have a variety and balance of fiction and informational text across many reading levels. • Books and resources are presented in displays and bins that support student self-selection. • A self-selection strategy and book bin protocol are posted and used by students in all classrooms. • Students have book bins or bags with several self-selected texts in them.
• Rituals, routines, and procedures are in place.	• All teachers have partnered with their students to create anchor charts or I-Charts that describe expectations for all aspects of instructional delivery. • Students transition from whole group to small group to independent work knowing rituals, routines, and procedures.
• Displays of student work show development and celebrate literacy learning. • Interactive word walls are used to support writing and vocabulary development.	• The walls of the classroom are "walls that teach." • A variety of examples of student work that honor effort and accomplishments are displayed. • Word walls are interactive, providing a visual scaffold that supports students' learning of sight words and/or vocabulary as they read and write.

in an intimate setting, such as convening on a carpeted area, can foster peer engagement opportunities. In addition, you'll need some small tables for small-group instruction, where groups of four to six students can work together. For independent reading and application time, students need places to comfortably read. Many teachers have a carpeted area near the classroom library to provide a relaxed and inviting area for reading. Ensuring that a classroom offers the spaces and places to move across these learning modalities—whole-group, small-group, and independent—is important.

Literacy-Focused Activities and Student Engagement

An important goal of a literacy-focused classroom is to engage students in authentic learning that will make them better readers, writers, thinkers, and problem solvers. Authentic, literacy-focused activities replicate real-life reading, writing, listening, and speaking purposes (Duke & Pearson, 2002) and require students to apply the learning explicitly taught and modeled by the teacher. When students are engaged in authentic learning activities, they are carefully reading and rereading with clear purposes, thinking analytically, and evaluating their understanding of texts and ideas orally or in writing (Schmoker, 2006).

Offering authentic learning opportunities in the classroom shifts student engagement from passive compliance—where students respond routinely and rely on the teacher to stay connected—to deep engagement, where students take full ownership of their learning and display high levels of interest and willingness to pursue answers and take risks in their learning (Fredericks, Blumenfeld, & Paris, 2004).

The Classroom Library

The classroom library is a critical resource in a balanced literacy classroom. A functional classroom library provides, at minimum, 12–20 books per student (International Reading Association, 2000; Newingham, 2015; Tyson, 2012) and consistent time to read them (Krashen, 2004). Texts need to be of high quality and represent a balance of fiction and informational text. E-books and audiobooks are also part of a rich classroom library. The books and resources should be organized to support student self-selection with a labeling system or through an arrangement in developmentally appropriate bins. A strong classroom library contains leveled texts, picture books, chapter books, books of various genres, content-area choices, and informational texts. Students know and use strategies for self-selection and have a process or protocol for assembling books for their independent reading time. See Figure 5.2 (p. 64) for a Classroom Library Checklist.

Rituals and Routines

The rituals, routines, and practices of an effective balanced literacy classroom provide the structure for students to become self-motivated, self-directed learners. The walls of the classroom speak to these important processes through anchor charts, posters, and other artifacts that identify the engagement and behaviors necessary during each aspect of the gradual release of responsibility. Students and teacher agree on what it will look like, sound like, and feel like to be doing their jobs during whole-group, small-group, and independent reading and application time. The class discusses the roles for teacher and students and records expectations on chart paper or some other visual display. The class establishes these rituals and routines during the first two to four weeks of school, as it is necessary to take some time to develop habits for effective participation and to build enough stamina to read daily for 20 to 30 minutes.

The Walls and Displays

A classroom's walls and displays can be used as dynamic teaching tools devoted to the display and study of words (Bear, Invernizzi, Templeton, & Johnston, 2000; Pinnell, Fountas, & Giacobbe, 1998). Interactive word walls encourage students to share what they notice about the features of a word, including how the word looks and sounds, what it means, and how it connects to other words. Word walls provide a visual scaffold to help students actively learn about words and use them in their daily writing and speaking.

Posted student work in progress as well as polished pieces can reflect the development of the community, tell the history of growth, and provide a context for the development of the class as learners (Anderson, 2011). Typically, although not always, student work displayed in the hall is finished and graded and represents students' best work. Student work in the classroom, on the other hand, is formative and used for learning. You and your students can decide what you wish to display to reflect the current learning and development happening in the classroom.

Classroom Visits Informed by Knowledge of Literacy Instruction

Understanding the approaches of balanced literacy and gradual release of responsibility is important while using the Literacy Classroom Visit instrument. This background knowledge enables leaders to review the specified data patterns while asking the following questions:

- Do the majority of classrooms in my school embody a culture that can successfully support literacy instruction?
- Is the literacy instruction in my school effective?
- Is the literacy instruction in my school balanced?
- Are teachers successfully releasing the responsibility for learning to their students?

Returning now to the full assessment instrument (see Figure 1.1, p. 14), we offer four examples of how knowledge of balanced literacy and gradual release of responsibility can help a leader identify areas of need during Literacy Classroom Visits.

Example 1. If the data patterns from classroom visits indicate that whole-group instruction dominates classroom time, then (1) teachers may not fully understand balanced literacy instruction, (2) teachers may believe that the best learning occurs when they are teaching, or (3) teachers' instructional focus may be on delivering content rather than teaching students.

Example 2. If the learning targets are posted in the majority of classrooms, but the performance criteria are not clearly articulated or demonstration of learning is not noted consistently, then (1) teachers may need more training and practice in writing and teaching with learning targets, (2) teachers may not fully understand that they must explicitly teach and model learning targets in order for students to learn content and independently apply their learning, or (3) teachers may need help knowing how the learning target can provide the vehicle for formative assessment across the gradual release of responsibility.

Example 3. If the majority of teachers are meeting with small groups at least 30 percent of class time but are not listening to students read or collecting data, then (1) teachers may not fully understand the importance of observing and listening to students read and apply their learning, (2) teachers may need additional training or support to change their stance from teacher to coach, or (3) teachers may need training or support to develop a system for data collection.

A classroom teacher with the expertise to support the teaching of reading to children having a variety of abilities and needs is the primary ingredient for reading success. (Snow, Griffin, & Burns, 2005, p. 11)

Example 4. If the data patterns show that independent reading or conferring is occurring minimally or not at all, then (1) teachers may need additional training in how to have students independently read self-selected texts, (2) teachers may need additional training in conferring with students so that they're able to observe students' ability to apply their learning while reading books of their own choice and to ascertain the degree to which students are mastering the learning, or (3) teachers may need experiences in applying the data from the conferences to help assess the success of the lesson and provide data for grouping students.

Delivery of Balanced Literacy Instruction

Once a community of educators understands the research base and philosophy of teaching balanced literacy across the gradual release of responsibility model, it can identify the mode of instructional delivery that they wish to use. Some educators might refer to this delivery mode as the curriculum. However, we define *curriculum* as the means and materials with which students will interact to achieve identified educational outcomes (Ebert, Ebert, & Bentley, 2013). Curriculum is made up of all the *planned and unplanned* experiences that the teacher orchestrates to ensure that students grow at least one grade level in every area each year (Bruner, 1960).

The delivery methods most common to supporting the gradual release of balanced literacy instruction are use of a basal or anthology series, a Reader's/Writer's Workshop Model, and the Daily 5/CAFE Model. These methods have similarities and differences, but success with any of them depends on the classroom culture and instructional components outlined in the Literacy Classroom Visit Model. Regardless of which delivery method is used, the LCV Model can help leaders gather meaningful data about areas of strength and need.

Knowing What to Look For: The Basics

3

Monitoring a school literacy program is a systematic process of examining students' literacy progress and teachers' instructional strategies. Effective monitoring practices are necessary for maintaining a quality literacy environment.

—Debra Johnson and Mary Foertsch,
Critical Issue: Monitoring the School Literacy Program

The Literacy Classroom Visit Model has several instruments in its tool kit: teacher surveys, the Literacy Classroom Visit instrument, and the resources for presenting the process to staff, which we discuss in Chapter 4. These tools serve as a way for leaders to introduce the elements of the process to educators involved in the LCV Model, to create understanding and gain buy-in throughout the school community, and to collect initial data around six key areas: classroom environment and culture, learning target/instructional goal, whole-group explicit instruction, small-group guided practice, independent reading and application, and student interaction and understanding. These initial steps create a solid foundation for a system of Literacy Classroom Visits that provide ongoing data about literacy instruction.

After administering the teacher survey and reviewing the data, it became apparent that we had a knowing/doing gap at our school. These survey data guided our planning for professional learning and helped us determine a focus for our classroom visits.

Dr. Janet Fawcett, Principal

The Teacher Survey

Leaders who are preparing to implement the Literacy Classroom Visit Model in their schools generally have two questions: (1) *How do I begin?* and (2) *How do I get buy-in from my staff?* Generally speaking, teachers demonstrate greater buy-in and participation when leaders explain concepts briefly, build on existing practices, allow time for reflection, and present themselves as a part of the learning process (Margolis, 2008). Accordingly, we have found that the best way to introduce the model is to invite teachers to a short meeting that gives a general overview of the LCV Model. In this meeting, you can explain that the school is introducing a new process in teachers' professional learning and that you want to build a partnership with them to determine the most effective literacy practices currently being used in the school as well as identify the resources and professional learning that can best foster student literacy achievement.

Then you can administer the Teacher Balanced Literacy Survey (see Figure 3.1, also available online; see note on p. 5) as a vehicle for teachers to share what they already know and do. Its purpose is threefold: (1) to provide time for teachers to reflect and build an understanding of the components of effective literacy instruction, (2) to enable you to compare teacher self-assessment with the data subsequently collected using the LCV instrument, and (3) to create an opportunity to discuss the data from the teachers' responses to the survey and how they contribute to the overall knowledge of instructional delivery. In Chapter 4, we discuss the initial meeting and teacher survey in more depth.

Figure 3.1 | *Teacher Balanced Literacy Survey*

DIRECTIONS: Reflect on your current level of understanding of the Balanced Literacy Gradual Release Model of Reading Instruction. Consider your current level of knowledge and understanding of each practice and select **one** option from the *understanding* column. Next, consider how often you integrate these practices into your teaching by selecting **one** option from the *use* column.

DESCRIPTION	UNDERSTANDING				USE			
	None or limited	Developing	Proficient	Expert	Rare or nonexistent	1–2 times/**week**	1–2 times/**month**	Daily
Classroom Environment and Culture								
1. I structure my classroom to support the gradual release of responsibility by providing space and movement for whole and small group and independent reading and application.								
2. My classroom library includes more than 300 texts equally representing fiction and informational texts and is organized to support student self-selection.								
3. My students and I have agreed-upon rituals, routines, and procedures and have developed anchor charts or other visible supports to ensure clear expectations.								
4. I display developing student work to celebrate growth and share the growing literacy skills of the class.								
Learning Target/Instructional Goal								
5. I post learning targets/goals that are aligned to standards and written in student-friendly language.								
6. My learning targets include clear explanations of what students will be expected to DO as a result of the lesson(s).								
7. I teach and assess my learning targets across the gradual release of responsibility.								
Whole-Group Explicit Instruction (Teacher is teaching)								
8. I teach focused mini-lessons that use time effectively for my students' age range.								
9. I explicitly teach and model effective skills and strategies with learning targets to set my students up for group and independent work.								
10. I use strategies to engage students during whole-group instruction that enable me to quickly assess understanding.								

Continued

Figure 3.1 | *Teacher Balanced Literacy Survey* (continued)

DESCRIPTION	UNDERSTANDING				USE			
	None or limited	Developing	Proficient	Expert	Rare or nonexistent	1–2 times/**week**	1–2 times/**month**	Daily
Small-Group Guided Practice (Teacher is coaching)								
11. I extend the explicit instruction and modeling from whole-group lessons by coaching students' reading, strategy application, and collaborative discussions.								
12. I listen to students read one-on-one (while other students read silently) to monitor their reading development and assess their application of the learning target.								
13. I have a record-keeping system to record data on students reading and applying their learning.								
14. My students read and discuss texts at their instructional level and practice the skills and strategies of the learning targets that were explicitly taught in whole group.								
Independent Reading and Application								
15. I provide 30 minutes of independent reading time for students to read self-selected texts.								
16. I confer one-on-one with students about their self-selected books, assessing their development and recording data.								
17. My students have a strategy to self-select a variety of books for independent reading to keep in a bin or bag as well as a way to record/log their reading.								
18. After reading for 30 minutes, students work on other rich activities that support the development of reading, writing, listening, and speaking skills.								
Data Collection and Use								
19. I have a record-keeping system to document my students' reading development.								
20. I use the data I collect about my students to review and revise my instruction, design lessons, and group students.								

Source: © 2014 by Bonnie D. Houck, EdD, and Sandi Novak. Used with permission.

The Literacy Classroom Visit Instrument

The Literacy Classroom Visit instrument provides the means to collect a wealth of evidence from every classroom around the aforementioned six key areas: classroom environment and culture, learning target/instructional goal, whole-group explicit instruction, small-group guided practice, independent reading and application, and student interaction and understanding. In Chapter 2, we looked at exemplary data for classroom environment and culture (see Figure 2.2, p. 24). Let's turn now to the other five key areas. Within the discussion of each of these areas, we include a table that lists the relevant classroom look-fors in the left column and a set of data as they might look across an exemplary school in the right column.

The use of the Literacy Classroom Visit instrument was beneficial for identifying trends and patterns throughout the school. As a principal, I could use the data gathered to determine purchasing and staffing decisions, as well as address professional development needs. The nonjudgmental emphasis was refreshing in this era of intense evaluation, rating, and ranking.

Dr. Julie Davis, Executive Director,
Ohio Association of Elementary Administrators

The Instructional Delivery Components

Four of the six key areas covered by the Literacy Classroom Visit instrument focus on instructional delivery: learning target/instructional goal, whole-group explicit instruction, small-group guided practice, and independent reading and application. Each component is an important part of the gradual release of responsibility and requires focus and reflection. Throughout the following sections, we show how these components might be integrated in a 5th grade classroom to help you view balanced literacy across the gradual release: from whole-group instruction to small-group guided practice to independent reading and application. The process starts with the learning target.

Learning target/instructional goal. A learning target (Moss, Brookhart, & Long, 2011) is a statement of intended learning for students based on the standards. It specifies and unpacks the objective and spells out what students will be able to do *during* and *after* the lesson or lesson series. A learning target is written in student-friendly language, is specific to the lesson for the day or span of days, and is directly connected to assessment. It includes performance criteria that outline what a student needs to know or do to demonstrate understanding. The teacher can assess students' level of mastery through observation, conferring, or evaluation using a rubric, a checklist, or other criteria. Figure 3.2 depicts the learning target data of an exemplary school.

Figure 3.2 | *Learning Target/Instructional Goal: What It Looks Like*

LCV Look-Fors in a Classroom	Across an Exemplary School
• Learning target/goal is posted in student-friendly language. • Learning target/goal identifies demonstration of learning (performance criteria). • Learning target/goal is taught and monitored across the gradual release of responsibility.	• The learning target is clearly posted in the majority of classrooms. • The majority of the learning targets identify performance criteria so that students understand what they are supposed to do and show as a result of instruction and practice. • The teacher weaves the learning target through all aspects of instructional delivery. • When asked, students can explain the learning target or what they are supposed to learn, do, and show.

The learning target for our sample 5th grade lesson is "I can adjust or change my thinking as I read independently and later talk within my group about the text, explaining how my thinking changed." This learning target is written in student-friendly language, is posted visibly, and outlines performance criteria. Students know what they are expected to know, learn, do, and show to demonstrate their mastery of the target.

Whole-group explicit instruction. During whole-group sessions, the teacher's role is to, well, teach! After introducing the learning target, the teacher unpacks the content and explains the performance criteria. The teacher may read a mentor text to provide an example of good writing and model several think-aloud examples of how to meet the performance criteria. Exemplary teachers directly and explicitly model the thinking and strategy application that skilled readers engage in when they decode a word, self-monitor for understanding, clarify meaning, and summarize while reading. Such teachers also foster engagement by encouraging interaction among all class members, and they design ways to quickly assess the level of understanding in the group through student responses, such as think-pair-share or whiteboard responses. When students are released from whole group, they clearly understand how they will practice the learning in small groups and apply it on their own with their independent reading texts or in some other application. This method of instruction looks quite different from the "assign and assess" approach that dominates in less effective classrooms (Adams, 1990; Durkin, 1978). Figure 3.3 shows what such practices would look like across an exemplary school.

Figure 3.3 | *Whole-Group Explicit Instruction: What It Looks Like*

LCV Look-Fors in a Classroom	Across an Exemplary School
• Teacher is leading a focused mini-lesson or lesson using time effectively for age range. • Teacher is explicitly teaching/modeling effective skill/strategy (learning target). • Students are actively listening, purposefully engaged, and interacting with the teacher. • Students are actively listening, purposefully engaged, and interacting with peers.	• Whole-group instruction is being done in a portion of the classrooms visited (balancing instructional time among whole-group, small-group, and independent instructional experiences). • The majority of teachers are explicitly teaching and modeling the performance criteria while thinking aloud about the thought processes and meaning making that skilled readers employ while reading. • The vast majority of students in every classroom appear to be listening and are responding to the teacher and peers to support their learning. • When teachers provide directions, students respond promptly and are able to follow through. • Although much of the interaction is between teacher and students, student-to-student interactions are also observed in many classrooms.

Let's return to our 5th grade classroom, where the teacher uses an interactive read-aloud to demonstrate her thinking around the learning target. She provides scaffolding by sharing a sentence frame that students can use to take notes on things they read that change their thinking ("I used to think...but my thinking has changed to..."). The teacher also describes how the discussion might sound when students organize themselves in their student-led small groups.

After the teacher uses a couple of short turn-and-talk moments to assess students' understanding of the learning target during the mini-lesson, she releases them to read their self-selected books independently, practicing and applying the learning target and noting how the unfolding text causes them to rethink and change their ideas. Later, they will share and discuss these changes with peers in their small groups. This whole-group lesson sets students up for success and takes up to 20 minutes.

A leader using the LCV instrument to observe this whole-group portion of the lesson can move through the learning target and whole-group sections of the LCV during a three- to five-minute classroom visit. The instrument focuses and guides the leader's observation and ensures that he or she notes effective aspects of literacy instruction. When the leader uses it in all classrooms across the school, he or she will be able to see which components are consistently taught and maintained while also noting areas in need of support.

Small-group guided practice. During the small-group step of the gradual release, the teacher's role is to coach and guide students' reading of instructional-level texts. Figure 3.4 shows what an exemplary school's data might look like for this category of instructional delivery.

Figure 3.4 | *Small-Group Guided Practice: What It Looks Like*

LCV Look-Fors in a Classroom	Across an Exemplary School
• Teacher is guiding students' reading, strategy application, and collaborative discussions. • Teacher is listening to students read individually while others read quietly. • Teacher is assessing strengths/needs and collecting anecdotal notes. • Students are reading and discussing texts at their instructional level. • Students are practicing the skill or strategy explicitly taught and modeled in whole group.	• The majority of teachers are coaching and supporting small groups of students reading texts. • In classrooms where students are silently reading in small groups, the teacher is listening to each student read and is actively taking notes about students' progress. • After the reading, the teacher prompts deep discussions about the text using higher-order questioning. • In some classrooms, student-led discussions are taking place; students follow a framework or protocol to guide their discussions. • In classrooms where students are leading their own small-group discussions, the teacher is actively observing and taking notes as students discuss texts. • In many classrooms, students work together in pairs as they discuss their texts. • Students are applying strategies taught in whole group with their peers in small groups.

In our 5th grade classroom, students work with peers, either under the guidance of their teacher or on their own, to practice the learning shared in whole group and apply other literacy skills and strategies. After giving students time to read and prepare during the whole-group phase, the teacher asks them to convene in their small groups to talk about the book they had read and practice the learning target taught in whole group. They are grouped in teams of four or five according to which book they had selected. Students share their notes, ideas, and textual evidence and discuss how their thinking has changed. As they listen to one another, their thinking continues to develop, resulting in creating deeper meaning about the text.

Working with each small group in turn, the teacher listens to students read, offers prompts and supports as students discuss their learning, and collects data about students' conversations and their application of the learning. Later, she provides feedback to groups and a few individuals about their growth and development.

The teacher also observes student-led small groups that practice a protocol she had taught and modeled for meeting with peers to discuss texts and ideas. She notes how well each group is working, the content of its conversation, and group members' ability to apply the learning, and she provides feedback to individuals as well as to the group.

The student-led discussion takes up to 20 minutes. Other grade-level examples and video clips of student-led discussions can be found in *Student-Led Discussions: How Do I Promote Rich Conversations About Books, Videos, and Other Media?* (Novak, 2014).

Independent reading and application. Expert teaching requires knowing not only how to teach strategies explicitly but also how to foster transfer from structured practice to independent use. During independent reading and application, the teacher's role is to confer, observe, assess, and collect data. Figure 3.5 shows what such practices would look like across an exemplary school.

Students in all classrooms who are reading independently during the literacy block should be reading self-selected texts for up to 30 minutes every day. Students' primary purposes during this time are to develop a love of reading and to become strategic readers by practicing the skills and strategies learned in whole group and practiced in small group while reading a variety of texts ranging across their independent through instructional reading levels. The teacher meets one-on-one with students to discuss their texts, ensure that they are self-selecting books that are a good fit, assess their level of mastery of the learning targets, and determine the level of their development as readers. Teachers also meet with students to confer about their ability to choose appropriate texts and their overall reading, writing, and language development. During this independent reading and application time, students may also be working on writing, word work, and other literacy-focused activities.

Figure 3.5 | *Independent Reading and Application: What It Looks Like*

LCV Look-Fors in a Classroom	Across an Exemplary School
• Teacher is conferring one-on-one with reader, assessing development, and recording data. • Students are reading self-selected books from a bag or bin and applying strategies learned. • Students are conferring with teacher about reading skills and/or demonstrating learning target. • Students are actively working at some other connected literacy enhancement activity.	• Most teachers who are not instructing whole group or meeting in small groups are actively conferring with individual students. • Teachers record data as they confer with students. • While conferring with students, teachers check students' fluency, comprehension, motivation and interest, goal setting, and strategy application. • All students have bags or bins or some method of keeping self-selected texts in a tool kit to be used for independent reading and conferring. • In many classrooms, students take the lead in their conferences, demonstrating their learning and application of strategies. • Students in many classrooms write in their response journals or write on sticky notes and place them in their books. • Students are able to answer the teachers' questions; many students elaborate when questioned about the text they are reading. • Most students are either writing or reading independently; very little work other than authentic reading or writing is observed.

Back in the 5th grade classroom, students extend their understanding of the learning target by applying their learning as they read their self-selected texts independently. As they read, the teacher confers one-on-one about how the characters and events in the stories they are reading may change. Each student takes the lead and shares his or her experience in applying the learning target with this or another book choice while the teacher determines whether the student has met the learning target. As the teacher reviews her data from conferring, she can determine whether the majority of students have met the learning goal and use these data to evaluate her lesson and inform future grouping and reteaching.

 Watch **Videos 3.1, 3.2,** and **3.3** to see how a 4th grade teacher uses the gradual release of responsibility to teach a learning target during a language arts lesson. Video 3.1 illustrates the whole-group lesson portion, during which the teacher models how to make an inference about a character, followed by guided and independent practice of the learning target. Video 3.2 links small-group guided reading with the whole-group lesson featured in Video 3.1. In Video 3.3, the teacher assesses the application of the learning target modeled in Video 3.1 by conferring with individual students.

The Final Component: Student Interaction and Understanding

Literacy instruction is a partnership between the teacher and students, so it is important to connect with students to assess their understanding. The teacher ensures that the learning targets are woven through the gradual release from whole group to small group to independent learning applications. If students don't understand this process, they won't be able to meet the learning goals.

When possible during a Literacy Classroom Visit, the leader should briefly speak with two or three students to determine how well they understand the learning target or lesson goal and what they are supposed to know, learn, do, and show. It is important to determine whether students know what they are learning and why, as well as teach them how to self-assess if their work meets expectations and what to do if they need help. Figure 3.6 shows what an exemplary school's data might look like for this important component.

Figure 3.6 | *Student Interaction and Understanding: What It Looks Like*

LCV Look-Fors in a Classroom	Across an Exemplary School
• Students can explain the learning target/ skill/strategy. • Students know what they are supposed to learn and how they are expected to demonstrate that learning in whole group or small group or on their own.	• When asked, students can clearly explain what they are learning. • When asked, students can clearly explain what they need to do and show to demonstrate their learning. • Students refer to the posted learning target while explaining their learning and the performance criteria. • Students are observed practicing the learning target in small groups and on their own.

Becoming Familiar with the Instrument

The Literacy Classroom Visit instrument is designed to be used during brief, frequent visits, so it does not review every possible element of literacy instruction. What it does do is help leaders collect data on the areas that are key to creating a motion picture (i.e., one that is created over a span of time) of the literacy culture and instruction in a learning community.

Before you set up your process and system for Literacy Classroom Visits, you need to become comfortable with the components explained in these first three chapters. Review the Balanced Literacy Gradual

Release Model of Reading Instruction document (Figure 2.1, p. 22) and the Literacy Classroom Visit instrument (Figure 1.1, p. 14). Think about what you will be looking for with regard to each of the six key areas of effective literacy instruction covered by the instrument. To understand the data that you will be gathering, review the exemplary school data for all these areas, handily compiled in Appendix A (pp. 123–140). If you have questions about any section of the instrument, review the discussion of that section in the text.

Ask a few teacher leaders if you can practice using the instrument in their classrooms. This will help you become comfortable with the components and hone your timing so that you can record data during three- to five-minute classroom visits. Decide if you wish to use an electronic format of the instrument or if you prefer to begin with a hard copy. Once you are familiar with the instrument and the process, you can begin to plan for implementation of the Literacy Classroom Visit Model.

Reflection to Action

1. How might the Literacy Classroom Visit Model align with the improvement efforts that you are incorporating in your school?
2. In what ways can the literacy culture in your school be strengthened?
3. How well do you understand the different sections and the look-for statements in the Literacy Classroom Visit instrument? What do you need to help you use this resource as effectively as possible?

PART II:
Putting the LCV Process into Action

SCENARIO: BLUFF CREEK ELEMENTARY SCHOOL

Initially, teachers thought I was conducting Literacy Classroom Visits to observe their individual teaching rather than to try to understand the current literacy practices across the school. After a few insightful discussions about effective balanced literacy practices, my teachers now look at these visits as opportunities to discuss what they do and why they are doing it. Several have commented about how these visits have created a partnership between themselves and our leadership team in supporting student learning.

One of the many positive areas of instructional change resulting from the LCV process has been the evolution of teacher reading conferences with students. Although we had professional development to support conferencing and collecting data using running records, teachers were not integrating this practice into their instruction. After collaborative discussions about the purpose of this important component of literacy instruction and focused training in conferring and data collection, many of our teachers are embracing these conferences as opportunities to learn about student reading development. Now, our teachers are actively gathering informal reading information about their students on a weekly basis and using the data to help identify and address specific needs.

The Literacy Classroom Visits in my school have evolved, and the outcomes include enriched instructional discussions, focused professional development, increased trust in leadership, and an increase in specific instructional changes throughout my school. I wholeheartedly recommend that principals consider Literacy Classroom Visits for three reasons:

(1) you will achieve a better understanding of both the successful and the developing elements of your literacy program; (2) your professional development for teachers will become more focused; and (3) the ongoing data gained through the process will support meaningful conversations about instructional strategies and learning happening in the school.

Our PLC work has become more profound as teachers explore literacy practices, respond to feedback from the visits, and share instructional strategies. As a principal, I am able to see how the resources we invest in classrooms are affecting student learning. Through these visits, I feel more connected to student learning and empowered to support my teachers in more meaningful ways.

One of my more vocal teachers had a recent "aha" moment that affirmed to me that we are heading in the right direction. During a discussion on conferring, she proclaimed, "I know more about my students' reading now than ever before!"

Joan MacDonald, Principal
Bluff Creek Elementary School
Chanhassen, Minnesota

Implementing the Literacy Classroom Visit Model

In a review of schools that have quickly improved student achievement, principals who conducted reading walkthroughs modeled strong leadership for instructional change.

—Rebecca Herman and colleagues,
Turning Around Chronically Low-Performing Schools

In this chapter, we provide direction for implementing Literacy Classroom Visits through a step-by-step overview of how to prepare for the visits, how to conduct the visits, how to reflect on the visits afterward, and how to plan next steps.

Before the Literacy Classroom Visits: Getting Ready

Before implementing a series of Literacy Classroom Visits, it is important to share and be transparent about the purpose, process, and particulars of the LCV Model. The principal, as the instructional leader, identifies the purpose for the Literacy Classroom Visits and thinks about a delivery plan that outlines what will happen before, during, and after the visits, along with the roles and responsibilities of all educators involved. When describing the LCV Model, the leader must be well versed and confident in the process. The following sections outline the steps leaders can take to prepare for implementation.

Individualize the Purpose

The overall purpose for the Literacy Classroom Visit Model is clear: to support continuous improvement in literacy instruction and learning and to promote inquiry and reflective practice focused on student growth and achievement. However, each school has its own culture and unique needs. Some schools may already have established a strong literacy culture and effective instructional practices and just need ideas for enhancement. Other schools are just beginning to develop a balanced literacy culture and need ways to cultivate all six key areas described in the LCV instrument. The LCV Model is flexible and can be used by any school interested in augmenting its literacy efforts. Therefore, it is important for leadership teams to clearly individualize the process and identify the purpose for each round of visits to align with their school's special needs.

Prepare the Staff

Literacy Classroom Visits are designed with the assumption that teachers will do their best for students if they understand what they need to do and they receive the necessary support, resources, and professional experiences. The LCV process involves all teaching staff, together with specialists who serve in supportive roles, such as the psychologist and social workers. Understanding the purpose and process of LCV and involving all staff in pre- and postdiscussions about the data and overall learning foster a collaborative school environment with common expectations for teaching and learning.

With the teacher survey administered at the beginning of the project, we found out our teachers' knowledge and use of best practices. The Classroom Library Checklist [see Figure 5.2, p. 64] informed us about our students' ability to have ready access to rich, varied classroom collections of books and other media. The LCV instrument is a resource that allows staff to better understand the direction we are headed because they know that I and others will be looking for the things listed on the form in their teaching and student learning. Then, so it isn't a "gotcha," we provide professional learning and resources to enhance their practices.

Dr. Steven Geis, Principal

Hold an Initial Staff Meeting

Research (Leithwood, 2002; Schwartzbeck, 2002) supports the importance of staff buy-in to the success of any school change or professional learning project. As we mentioned in Chapter 3, we have found that the best way to cultivate buy-in and develop a common vision for the school's literacy culture is to hold a staff meeting explaining the LCV process and how it fits with the work currently being done in the school and district. We'll now explain the method and resources that many principals have found helpful when explaining the LCV process to teachers. To get a look at the process in action, see **Video 4.1**, which shows a staff meeting in which a principal and literacy coach share the LCV process, and **Video 4.2**, in which five principals from one school district share how they informed their staffs about the LCV Model and describe their teachers' reactions.

You can begin the staff conversation by sharing "Literacy Classroom Visits in a Nutshell," found in Appendix A (pp. 123–140), and allowing teachers time to read, discuss, and ask questions about the purpose and process of LCVs. This positive, open communication reduces potential anxiety and encourages teachers to ask questions. Explain the purpose of the visits, when the visits will begin, who will be participating, and the methods that will be used to share the data from the visits. This communication ensures that teachers clearly understand that LCVs are designed to identify patterns of strength and need across the school—not to evaluate individuals. Once teachers have a greater understanding of the process, they usually look forward to discussing what the data may reveal and how new resources and learning can support students' reading development.

Another helpful resource for explaining the LCV Model is the Balanced Literacy Gradual Release Model of Reading Instruction (Figure 2.1, p. 22). Using this resource, teachers can discuss the important components of literacy instruction and share areas of strength with their colleagues.

After this initial discussion, share the LCV instrument (Figure 1.1, p. 14) and model the connection between the research-supported instructional components of balanced literacy and the "look-for" elements on the LCV instrument. To ensure that teachers feel confident in their understanding of each look-for component, you can share "Discussing the Components of Literacy Classroom Visits" (Appendix A, pp. 123–140).

These resources help prepare teachers for the visits and ensure that they know why they are regularly occurring, what LCV teams will be looking for, and how the information will be used.

Survey the Staff

Depending on time constraints, you can introduce the Teacher Balanced Literacy Survey (Figure 3.1, pp. 31–32) at this initial meeting or at a future meeting. This survey provides teachers with the opportunity to reflect on their own instructional practices and beliefs about literacy instruction and guides self-assessment of their individual strengths and needs. The survey also serves as a development tool, giving teachers time to reflect deeply on the look-for components of the instrument and consider how they are integrating them into their own classrooms.

Principals using this tool report that their teachers appreciate learning that the survey data will help inform the administration about staff resource and professional learning needs. When teachers know they will be included in the reflective practices and decision-making processes that have a direct effect on their practice and on students, they realize that their voice and choice matter.

Identify the Method of Data Collection

The Literacy Classroom Visit instrument and the Teacher Balanced Literacy Survey can be used in either hard-copy or electronic format. (These resources are available online for download; see note on p. 5.) The electronic format makes the process easier in some ways: the data arrays and charts it yields can relay important data visually and numerically. In addition, as you move through the LCV Model, you will be reassessing your classroom visit focus over time to meet the evolving needs of your staff and students. The electronic format makes this data collection and retrieval process easier.

If you choose to use hard-copy forms, consider the best way to collect the data. Collecting and reviewing data by completing one hard-copy form per classroom may be confusing, and it's a time-consuming method to note patterns across the whole school. For a consolidated process, we offer the Literacy Classroom Visit Whole-School Instrument in our selection of online resources, which provides the opportunity to collect and review data from several classrooms using one form. Choose the method that will work best for your school team.

Convene the LCV Team

Many principals want to try out the LCV instrument alone or with another leader to become familiar and confident with it before asking others to join the process. Although this isn't wrong, it is crucial to include teachers in the process over time, since they provide an important voice and perspective. Inviting teachers to participate in LCVs

1. Builds a collaborative process that engages teachers and administrators in working together toward instructional improvement.
2. Results in greater clarity of purpose, a shared vision of effective practice, and a shared commitment to specific improvement initiatives.
3. Enhances the credibility of the process and increases support from the staff.

Literacy Classroom Visits can be an excellent team process. Initially, you might want to select team members who represent each grade level or content area of the teaching staff. Teams may also include school or district leaders, such as literacy coaches, reading specialists, or the professional development coordinator. Some principals partner with colleagues from other buildings and develop a collaborative team among two or three schools. As teams develop their confidence and competence in doing the visits, they can conduct visits without the principal. Developing a variety of ways to collect data using LCVs broadens the context for the data, inspires rich conversations, and builds collaboration.

Train the LCV Team

All team members should be trained in the LCV process so that they have a common understanding of how the day will work and which area their data collection should focus on. By receiving this training before the day of the LCV, the team can focus on data collection during the LCV without getting bogged down in figuring out the process. This training (see **Video 4.3** to view a facilitator orienting a team through the LCV materials and the agenda) should include

- Norms for group participation and a protocol for visiting class-rooms (see "Literacy Classroom Visit Protocol" in Appendix A, pp. 123–140).
- The area of focus and data collection instrument and component summary (see Figure 1.1 and "Discussing the Components of Literacy Classroom Visits" [Appendix A, pp. 123–140]).
- The guidelines for collecting data and debriefing the classroom visits.
- The schedule for the day and other related logistics.

Develop a focus. A critical step in the LCV process is to develop an area of focus that defines what teams look for in their classroom visits. Clearly defining the lens for collecting evidence is necessary for ensuring that LCVs will help educators set priorities and guide improvement efforts.

The initial purpose for the visits is usually to gather baseline data about the developing culture and instructional practices in the school. Consequently, team members should use the LCV instrument to look at general literacy practices. Over time, as the data pinpoint areas of need, the focus will narrow—for example, to just whole-group teaching and learning or just independent reading and application. We introduce additional instruments in subsequent chapters that teams can use to address and collect data for these specific areas of focus. Using the LCV instrument and refining the area of focus as new data emerge can provide valuable insight into the degree to which existing improvement efforts are taking root in the classroom. This process can help shape subsequent improvement planning.

Review all documents. After identifying the area of focus, decide whether you plan to use one LCV instrument for each classroom or the LCV Whole-School Instrument. The whole-school form allows all data to be collected in one place. Some leaders also consider transferring the content of the LCV instrument into an electronic data collection tool. The important thing is to choose the process that works best for your team members as they gain mastery in using the LCV Model. Whichever path you choose, this is a good time to review all the documents with your LCV team to ensure that team members understand and can identify each look-for component in a classroom. For the first round of classroom visits, conversations usually center on reviewing the LCV instrument and "Discussing the Components of Literacy Classroom Visits" (Appendix A, pp. 123–140). A common understanding of each component strengthens the fidelity and consistency among different team members' observations and data collection.

After discussing the components of the instrument during the visits and ensuring that the team has an understanding of each component, you can share "Literacy Classroom Visit Protocol" (Appendix A, pp. 123–140), the schedule, and the communication methods that will be used throughout the process.

I have looked more closely at our school's literacy practices and identified specific components for improvement. The classroom visits were more enjoyable and effective than others I have done in the past. I gained an overview of the needs of the whole system versus focusing on individual teacher improvement. I want to continue to learn about the change process in relation to implementing a strong and unified balanced literacy block in all classrooms.

Phil Gurbada, Principal

Collect data, not judgments. Data collection and note taking provide the evidence that serves as the basis for later discussion, so it's crucial that they're high-quality. Specific and objective notes generate richer and more focused discussions than do general or judgmental observations. The facilitator, who may be the principal or the literacy leader, helps team members focus on stating factual evidence, such as "I heard . . ." and "I saw . . .", and refrain from subjective statements, such as "I liked . . . " or "The teacher did a good job of . . ."

Develop a schedule. Initially, we suggest focusing on instruction during the literacy block, which means you need to schedule visits accordingly. When beginning the Literacy Classroom Visit Model in your school, it helps to share the schedule of your classroom visits with staff. Eventually, you can use a more spontaneous approach. Also, when conducting additional rounds of LCVs, be mindful to schedule visits at varying times during the literacy block. Because instruction at the beginning of the block is different from instruction during the middle or at the end of the block, observing instruction during these different times will yield better data.

If you have a lot of classrooms to visit, you may wish to divide the classrooms among the observers. If you decide to go this route, think about the continuity of your model: will the same people continue to visit the same classrooms to keep the data consistent? Or will you alternate so that each member of the team visits all the classrooms? How much time will teams spend in each classroom to establish consistency and reliability? How will you document a teacher's absence? Consider the possibilities that can affect the data collection and reach a consensus on your approach. Remember, this approach is about collecting broad data to see emerging patterns over time. Slight variants will not unduly affect the overall process, but every effort should be made to collect viable data.

Another point to consider is that it can be helpful to visit each grade level consecutively, noting impressions for one before moving to the next. Important observations about common practices, such as similar learning targets, aligned rituals and routines, and common conferring practices, can provide valuable insight into the level of cohesion and collaboration within grade-level teams. This method also can be helpful if a team of people is collecting data or you need to spread the visits across several days.

The LCV Model in Action: Autumn Ridge

Throughout the remainder of this chapter, we provide an ongoing example of one school's process of establishing the LCV Model in its overall continuous improvement plan. Autumn Ridge is a K–5 elementary school in a first-tier suburb of a large metropolitan area with four teachers per grade level. Dr. Castle, the principal, is an established instructional leader with a strong background in effective literacy instruction. She began to implement the LCV Model during her second year of leadership in this school.

Dr. Castle's plan for implementing the LCV Model began by collecting a round of initial baseline LCV data on her own before inviting a team of colleagues—principals from other schools—to join her in the data collection process and provide an objective view of the status of her school's literacy culture. These initial steps set the foundation for a smooth transition to using the LCV Model with teams of teachers from her school.

When it came time to begin the process of data collection with her school team, Dr. Castle felt confident and ready to lead because she had a few rounds of LCVs under her belt. Initially, one teacher from each grade level and a specialty teacher received LCV training prior to the team's first round of classroom visits. On the day of the first LCV with her school team, she developed a schedule listing the room numbers and times for each visit. The LCV team separated into two groups, with each group visiting two grade levels. The visits overlapped, with each classroom having two teams visiting during its literacy block. All visits concluded by noon, providing time in the afternoon to discuss the data.

During the Literacy Classroom Visits: Seeking the Story of Learning

This phase of the LCV Model presents a good opportunity to reflect on the data collected in the initial rounds and the overall strengths and needs of teachers and students, and to shape your plan for orienting all members of the larger team to the overall process. The following sections guide you as you plunge into implementation and seek the story of learning at your school.

Team Orientation

An orientation for team members on the day of an LCV provides an overview of the process and ensures fidelity to it. To make the most efficient use of time and ensure that all classroom visits occur during the teachers' literacy block, we recommend conducting the orientation before students arrive. The orientation should provide the schedule, the area of focus, the data collection instrument, the note-taking protocol, and the feedback process. It should also review what related work has already been done in the school. If previous LCVs have been conducted with the same area of focus, it is important to reflect on what was learned, any actions taken as a result, and the changes and improvements that may be emerging (see Video 4.3). This is also a good time to remind team members not to share feedback with anyone else or discuss the LCVs until the team has discussed the data together. This is critical to the overall success of your LCVs!

Begin the Visits

Equipped with the LCV instrument, begin the round of visits by going into one or two classrooms as a full team, then discussing what you saw and coming to an agreement about each component of the LCV instrument. This calibrates the data collection among the team members and ensures greater data reliability. After that first five-minute classroom visit, step into a nearby quiet area with your team and discuss what you noticed about the instruction being provided in the classroom. Compare notes on which components you believed were present and which seemed to be missing. Also discuss any anecdotal notes or evidence you wrote. (For a firsthand look at this process, see **Video 4.4**, which shows a team visiting the first classroom in an elementary school. To ensure the reliability of the instrument, they discuss the LCV look-fors they observed before they go on to collect data in other classrooms.) Once you agree on the data, you are ready to proceed to the next classroom. Continue visiting the rest of the classrooms without discussion between each visit.

One cautionary note: as we mentioned above, take care not to discuss classroom observations and data in the halls between classroom visits. If teachers see LCV team members talking about their visits or looking at their notes, they may suspect that they are being evaluated individually and feel skeptical about the whole LCV process. Thus, a seemingly harmless conversation among colleagues could end up sabotaging all the work you've done to ensure a nonevaluative process of observing teachers.

After the Literacy Classroom Visits: Understanding and Sharing the Story

After conducting the LCVs, team members have a great deal of information in their heads and on the instrument. They need time to organize their overall thoughts, review their data, and discuss those data with the team. It is important to build this time into the schedule, so that the debrief and discussion of data are effective. The following sections walk you through this process.

Reflect and Debrief

The discussion of evidence at the end of the day is the capstone of the LCV team experience. Once team members have engaged in individual reflection and review, they can participate in the debriefing session, discussing their observations, organizing information, and articulating insights gained from the process, with the goal of developing action steps to support teaching and learning.

The leader kicks off the discussion to model effective, nonevaluative observation and sharing. Next, the facilitator finds ways to ensure that all team members have an equal chance to share their observations and evidence. He or she helps the group put as many data on the table as possible and keeps the conversation limited to specific and objective evidence, redirecting people if the language becomes too general or judgmental. A good facilitator is wary of allowing broad generalizations based on a single day's worth of evidence and keeps the conversation from straying from the area of focus. Discussions continue by reviewing and discussing each of the six areas on the Literacy Classroom Visit instrument.

Identify Initial Data Patterns

Using the Data Analysis Framework Instrument (Appendix B, pp. 141–146) as a guide, revisit each of the six key areas and deeply analyze what you observed and learned. For each area, review and discuss the data collected and observations made during the visits, and then distill the findings to identify one or two areas of strength and need. Engage in reflective dialogue to determine the methods of support that could further develop the strengths or have a positive effect on the needs.

After discussing each of the six areas, consider which resources and professional development experiences would have the greatest effect on developing the area of need. Generate a list of possibilities and prioritize. Many districts have limited financial resources and specified professional development schedules, so discussion of further methods of data collection may be warranted in order to make the best decisions within these constraints. **Video 4.5** portrays a team talking about its LCV observations to determine patterns of strength and need.

The LCV Model in Action: Autumn Ridge

In the LCV team's debriefing of the initial classroom visits, data patterns emerged indicating several potential areas of focus, but the group analysis and discussion revealed that the most immediate need was to help teachers develop learning targets (see Figure 4.1). Although teachers had received some professional development on learning targets, the data indicated that they needed more support.

Figure 4.1 | *Autumn Ridge Elementary School's LCV Data*

Date: October 10, 2014	
Learning Target/Instructional Goal Look-Fors	**% of Classrooms**
Learning target/goal is posted in student-friendly language.	57%
Learning target/goal identifies demonstration of learning (performance criteria).	35%
Learning target/goal is taught and monitored across the gradual release of responsibility.	46%

Plan Staff Discussions and Communication

Current research (Goodwin & Miller, 2012) on classroom observations stresses that teachers should receive prompt feedback on the information gathered during an LCV. Sharing the results in a timely manner promotes schoolwide acceptance of the evidence as well as support for the resulting actions. Immediate communication with staff reduces uncertainty and can provide a valuable opportunity to demonstrate how the process is contributing to overarching school or district improvement efforts. The principal should always play a key role in this communication process, if not delivering the information directly.

The broad patterns emerging from the LCV process should also be shared with the district to inform thinking about systems and structures. District leaders can serve as an important source of support for resulting action steps. They may also have the capability of aggregating the LCV evidence across multiple schools in the district to draw powerful conclusions about patterns of practice and allocation of resources.

Initial analysis can illuminate some broad data patterns and begin to tell the story of a school's developing literacy culture, but a long-range, well-constructed plan of action requires deeper analysis. Before long-range planning, it is important to share the big-picture data with teachers to get an overall response. First, though, look at the data from the initial teacher survey and compare what teachers identified as key areas of strength and need with the initial analysis of the LCV data. Is there alignment or discrepancy between the two data sets? Did teachers overestimate their skill in integrating balanced literacy components into their daily practice? Did the LCV team find that teachers underestimated their abilities? The outcome of a conversation around these questions can help determine both what the team will share with teachers after the first round or two of data collection and the focus of the next round.

If the data align and there is not a great deal of discrepancy between the two data sets, communication with staff will be easier. However, we recommend that staff communication in the early stages of establishing your LCV Model be broad, general, and aligned to the resources and professional learning experiences you can provide. It is not appropriate or respectful to share data on areas of need that teachers do not have enough resources to address or that will not be targeted through professional development.

Generate Summary Statements

Once the LCV team reaches consensus on the data patterns revealed by the evidence, it should generate three to five summary statements that capture the most salient themes and are supported by specific evidence. For example, the data may indicate the school has well-organized classroom libraries set up for student self-selection in the vast majority of classrooms, but there is a need for more informational texts to ensure a balance of fiction and nonfiction. A possible action step would be to ask teachers to conduct a short inventory of their libraries to further identify the areas of need. In addition, the principal could provide a budget for ordering texts to fill in the gaps.

Another summary statement could be that although the data indicate that learning targets are posted, visible, and aligned to standards with relative frequency, performance criteria need to be clarified to better monitor student progress. The follow-up action might include exploring this area in a future PLC meeting.

Such summary statements describe instructional patterns gleaned from the review of evidence and can help focus and guide thinking around next steps. They should tell a meaningful story in a small number of statements that will be shared with the school community and fellow staff as a way to prompt further discussion and learning on the topic. It is essential that the team reach consensus on what to share and present the findings with a unified voice. If staff sense that there is dissent or disagreement among team members regarding the themes that emerged, the validity of the summary statements will be undermined. **Video 4.6** captures principals at a training sharing their summary statements after school teams had conducted LCVs in each of their schools.

The LCV Model in Action: Autumn Ridge

The following summary statements emerged from the Autumn Ridge LCV team's discussion:

- The three greatest strengths throughout the school that emerged from this round of LCVs were (1) classroom libraries are organized to support self-selection and support class size/level, (2) students are actively and purposefully engaged in literacy-focused learning activities, and (3) rituals, routines, and procedures are in place.

- An area of need that the data generated was in the writing, teaching, and assessing of learning targets. The data indicated that learning targets were posted in student-friendly language in 57 percent of classrooms, that the learning target identified demonstration of learning (performance criteria) in 35 percent of the classrooms, and that the learning target was taught and monitored across the gradual release of responsibility in 46 percent of the classrooms.

Following the LCV team's first round, Dr. Castle planned to meet with her literacy leadership team to determine action steps to address this area of need and explain to staff members how they would be supported as they worked to enhance this specific area.

Next Steps

After sharing the broad data with staff members and discussing their perceptions and reactions, use the data analysis to plan next steps. What will be the focus of the next round of LCVs? If you have decided to purchase resources and materials, will they affect classroom environment, culture, or instruction? If so, do you wish to focus on the first set of components in the LCV instrument? If you have provided professional learning opportunities, what changes or improvements in instructional practice do you expect to see, and when? Use the data analysis, your conversations with your staff, and your perceptions based on these data to plan your next round of visits.

The LCV Model in Action: Autumn Ridge

Over the next eight weeks following the initial LCV rounds, teachers met in teams to study the research supporting learning targets. They discussed the criteria required for creating effective learning targets and how to teach and assess them. They shared lesson plans and student work at their meetings. Then, the leaders from the original LCV team were invited back to revisit the classrooms. Although they used the same LCV instrument to collect data, the learning target area of observation was expanded to provide more specific data. These additional look-for elements were identified by the Autumn Ridge staff based on the criteria of effective learning targets that they had learned about in their professional learning sessions. Inviting and using teacher input in this way ensured inclusion of teacher voice in the LCV process.

Data revealed a significant improvement in the areas previously noted, and data for the newly added components were encouraging (see Figure 4.2). All classrooms had posted and visible targets, and nearly all were written in student-friendly language. The identification of performance criteria increased from 35 percent to 50 percent, and the teaching and assessing of the learning target increased from 46 percent to 53 percent. In the newly added areas of alignment to standards, what students will learn, and what students will demonstrate to show their learning, baseline data were at or above 50 percent.

Continued

Figure 4.2 | *Autumn Ridge Elementary School's Enhanced Learning Target Data*

Date: November 21, 2014

Learning Target/Instructional Goal Look-Fors	% of Classrooms
Learning target/goal is posted and visible in the learning area.	100%
Learning target/goal is written in student-friendly language.	93%
Learning target/goal is aligned to standards.	85%
Learning target/goal describes what students will learn by the end of the lesson.	66%
Learning target/goal identifies demonstration of learning (performance criteria).	50%
Learning target/goal is taught and monitored across the gradual release of responsibility.	53%

The data supported the effectiveness of the professional development and provided clear guidelines for teachers as well as laying out the next steps for professional learning in this area: teachers needed more practice in teaching, coaching, and assessing the learning targets and in turning the ownership for learning over to students.

Conclusion: Dr. Castle and her teachers were able to continue to share and analyze their learning targets, lesson plans, and student work and collaborate on strategies for continuous improvement because they initially gathered data using an instrument with clearly defined criteria. The meaningful sharing of ideas and experiences through the classroom visits from 12 instructional leaders helped all of them understand what good literacy instruction looks like in the classroom. These leaders couldn't wait to bring the model back to their own schools, have teachers become an integral part of the process, and understand ways to better support student learning and growth.

Data Analysis and Common Patterns

5

Making the continuous-improvement perspective and the processes of data-informed decision-making part of the way in which educators function requires a major cultural change. Such a change will not occur without leadership, effort, and well-designed supports.

—Barbara Means and colleagues,
Evaluation of Evidence-Based Practices in Online Learning

In this chapter, we show you how to dig deeper into the data, identify common patterns that need to be addressed, and enhance your LCV instrument to meet your school's specific, ongoing needs.

As we discussed in Chapter 4, the process of using data to plan for improvement begins by sharing and discussing the initial data with your teachers. We advise bringing a broad sample of data patterns, along with a tentative plan for attainable, *short-term* success, to teachers for their input and informing them that you will be sharing information throughout the process as they analyze data, make decisions, implement next steps, and collect further data using the LCV Model. Encouraging teacher input at pivotal points during the process lends transparency to the process and may yield important details about the process that assist you in making decisions. Doing this will also foster a collaborative environment in which teachers reflect on the critical components of balanced literacy instruction across the school community while simultaneously enhancing their own practices. To carry out this task successfully and ensure staff buy-in, it is important to

1. Resist sharing too many data too soon.
2. Carefully study the data to determine which goals can be accomplished in a short amount of time.
3. Identify the resources that will be needed to carry out the plan for improvement.

Time is always at a premium in education. Investing in this first step toward developing your Literacy Classroom Visit Model will form the foundation for deeper, more difficult work in the future.

Note that while the staff is tackling the initial goals, LCV team members continue to collect and analyze data. The Literacy Classroom Visit instrument was intentionally designed to focus on a school's overall literacy culture and the elements of effective instructional practices ingrained within that culture. If these components are actively integrated into daily teaching, then responsibility and ownership for learning will shift from teachers to students. Teachers will be actively observing student learning and collecting data to become better informed about their own teaching as well as student growth. While the LCV team continues to collect data using tools from the LCV Model, it creates a continuous-progress model of professional learning and teaching that is continually revised and differentiated to maintain the balance of challenge and success.

Identifying and Addressing Common Patterns

In Chapter 4, we shared the process of reviewing data to note areas of strength and need. Initially, the LCV instrument is used to gather baseline data about the status of literacy within the whole school. After a series of visits has been conducted using this instrument, certain patterns may appear that can be addressed with professional learning or additional resources (see the Autumn Ridge narrative in Chapter 4 for a real-life example).

The data generated from these LCVs will be unique, depending on your school's culture and teaching practices. That said, we have identified five patterns that commonly emerge from schools' LCV data. Some schools may have only one pattern, whereas other schools have multiple patterns. Watch **Video 5.1** for a look at principals talking about common patterns in LCV data.

Determining the emergent patterns in your data and prioritizing them based on need is an important part of the LCV Model. After your leadership team has identified a pattern that needs to be addressed at your school, you will want to refine the relevant section of the LCV instrument to address that particular area of focus. We provide a number of examples of enhanced LCV instruments, also known as "check-ins," to refer to as your team engages in this improvement process. Keep in mind that although it is important to use an instrument to examine the area of focus more closely, this instrument will not be effective unless professional learning and resources are allocated to address these needs. (Chapter 6 discusses professional development in greater depth.)

Pattern 1: Classroom Environment and Culture Are Not Consistent Across the School

In a classroom that supports balanced literacy instruction, a teacher uses the physical space, resources, and routines to create a climate of learning. The classroom's layout and flow can tell an observer whether there is a good balance between teacher-led and student-led learning. The classroom library is key, being the source for texts that students need for independent reading and application of learning. The number and types of texts, as well as how they are arranged, reveal the ease with which students can choose texts that best support their interests and learning needs. In addition, observing students engaged in authentic independent reading and writing activities informs the observer that the teacher is gradually releasing the ownership of learning to students. When learning tasks mirror real-world contexts, students are more motivated to learn and cognitive engagement is increased (Blumenfeld, Kempler, Krajcik, & Blumenfeld, 2006).

Data that show low incidences of established literacy rituals, routines, and procedures can indicate a need for greater structure in student-teacher interactions. Such data may also suggest that teachers see students as receivers of content rather than as partners in learning. The walls of the room and the type of student work displayed can tell the story of what kind of learning is valued. For example, in classrooms where displays of work show students' current learning and development, the emphasis is on growth and improvement rather than on mere completion. These elements help the observer consider the degree to which the classroom environment supports literacy learning.

Figure 5.1 shows data from a compilation of classroom visits in a school where the classroom environment and culture emerged as a key area of need. In this example, the LCV team used the Data Analysis Framework Instrument (Appendix B, pp. 141–146) to list strengths, needs, and possible ways to address those needs.

Figure 5.1 | *Example of Classroom Environment and Culture Data from Literacy Classroom Visits*

CLASSROOM ENVIRONMENT AND CULTURE
52% Students are actively and purposefully engaged in literacy-focused learning activities.
32% Classroom library is organized to support self-selection and class size/level (300+ texts).
16% Classroom library has a balance of fiction/informational texts at varied levels.
26% Rituals, routines, and procedures are in place (interactive I-Charts, process for book selection, etc.).
22% Displays of student work show development and celebrate literacy learning.
24% Interactive word walls are used to support writing and vocabulary development.
Comments: Many students working in workbooks or using packets. Literacy-focused activities observed about half of the time. Classroom libraries are present in all classrooms, but only about a third are organized for student self-selection. Texts are primarily fiction. Daily 5 and other anchor charts are found in about a quarter of classrooms, but consistent classroom management structure was not observed. Word walls posted in many primary classrooms, but interactive elements and alignment of word choice and number were not observed.

The data in Figure 5.1 indicate that only half of the students observed were actively and purposefully engaged in literacy-related activities during their literacy block. The classroom libraries need organization for self-selection as well as an infusion of informational texts to enable students to choose appropriate texts and practice the skills required in the English language arts standards. Three-quarters of the classrooms are in need of structured routines and practices to support a common language and common practices across grade levels. The data noted an overall lack of continuity and no unified philosophy.

To design systemic and sustained changes in classroom instruction and learning, a school must develop a clear focus and a common language that allow teachers to discuss and implement shared practices that set high standards for student performance (Schooling, Toth, & Marzano, 2013). Aligned practices and a common language ensure consistency in instruction.

Inconsistencies in classroom practices and instructional delivery may show up in numerous areas. Let's look at word walls as an example. An observer may find that grade-level teachers vary in their methods of displaying and using word walls. A teacher who uses the word wall to support the development of sight words and their application during reading and writing will have taught and posted words that correlate with reading goals. When the data indicate that each teacher is using different words or a different number of words on the walls, teachers may lack a common understanding of the purpose of the word wall. Another problem might be words displayed high on the wall, out of student reach, which would indicate a lack of expectation or process for using the words in daily reading and writing, thus informing observers that the word wall is static rather than interactive and does not support ongoing learning.

Such data create an overall picture of need that would be challenging for teachers to take in and digest in one meeting. Rather, the data indicate that teachers need professional development on how to set up the classroom environment to support balanced literacy instruction, with a focus on organizing strong classroom libraries and developing common practices, routines, and classroom management procedures. These areas require change in teachers' established practices. Because introducing changes too quickly may cause anxiety, we recommend that you use a two-step process.

Step 1: Improving classroom libraries. The first step is to develop organized classroom libraries. This is an effective way to begin because the task is manageable and can be addressed by adding some new resources and time. By investing in this process, you are demonstrating the importance of these efforts to the entire school community while offering an initial solution to address an identified need. Your partnership and support, along with the excitement of new resources, will arouse teachers' interest and ease their anxiety about change.

First, arrive at a budget that you can provide for teachers to purchase additional texts and resources to organize their libraries. Each teacher then works to identify the specific resources needed in his or her classroom library and converses with grade-level colleagues to align their resource purchases. To facilitate this process, teachers can use a checklist or self-reflection inventory, such as the Classroom Library Checklist in Figure 5.2.

Figure 5.2 | *Classroom Library Checklist*

Classroom Library Environment
☐ The classroom has a clearly designated, accessible, and inviting library space.
☐ The classroom has several areas for students to read comfortably.
☐ Classroom rituals and routines are established to support student self-management of independent reading.
☐ The library area has room for three to four students to review and select texts.

Classroom Library Content
☐ My classroom collection includes at least 300–600 texts.
☐ The selection includes a balance of fiction and informational texts.
☐ The selection includes a range of genres and text structures.
☐ The selection includes a range of levels that meet the needs of my students.
☐ The selection includes a variety of high-quality texts that are appropriate for students' age level, interests, and development.
☐ Texts have characters and content that are relevant to students' backgrounds and to the community.
☐ Many texts support content that students are learning (e.g., math, science, social studies).

Student Readiness and Self-Direction
☐ Students have been explicitly taught strategies for self-selection.
☐ Students have the stamina to read independently for up to 30 minutes.
☐ Students have a book bin/box and a protocol for selecting the content that goes in it.
☐ Students have a log or graph to record their reading and goals.

Organization and Management
☐ Shelves, bins, and containers display texts and promote self-selection.
☐ Texts are organized in multiple ways (e.g., by level, genre, picture or chapter book, favorite author).
☐ Students know the system of organization and use it effectively.
☐ Anchor charts provide guidance for self-selection, book bin protocols, and exchange of texts.
☐ Checkout and return system is in place and supports ongoing organization.
☐ The collection includes a system to "weed" old, unused books and "feed" new books.

Independent Reading and Conferring
☐ I have a conferring schedule to meet with students weekly or biweekly.
☐ I have a process for data collection.
My conferring sessions include regular use of
☐ Goal setting, which includes book choice, reading volume and/or pace, and reading of a variety of genres;
☐ A system to check strategy application; and
☐ Assessment of fluency and comprehension.

The Classroom Library Checklist provides a quick way for teachers to assess their overall library collection while reflecting on their overall classroom routines and instructional practices that support students' use of the classroom library. Using the data from this tool with the LCV analysis can guide teachers' conversations about their resource and professional learning needs and about how to develop their libraries to support students' independent reading and learning.

Step 2: Establishing consistent rituals and routines. The second step requires teachers to reflect more deeply on the classroom routines and management systems they use to support instruction, which may cause some anxiety. Therefore, it is crucial to provide the data and begin by discussing the rituals and routines that are currently working well. Then you can work with teachers to explore ways to develop areas of need while sharing professional development options that can extend areas of strength. Give teachers time to reflect, discuss, and share their input and ideas.

Pattern 2: Learning Targets Are Not Guiding Instruction

The term *learning target* may be new, but the idea that we need to construct measurable goals for learning and make them visible and understandable to students has long been the foundation of effective instruction. Before teaching, we must know what goal we plan to teach and why it is important for students to learn it. We need to determine what students will do to develop knowledge and understanding of the goal and how they will demonstrate that understanding. Once we have established our goals for teaching and learning, we explicitly teach and model the outcome and provide time for students to practice the learning in supportive situations, both with peers and on their own. During this release of responsibility, we monitor students' progress and scaffold support for those who need reinforcement while offering extension for those who need more challenge. This practice exemplifies effective teaching in every subject area.

In literacy, where fluency, comprehension, and vocabulary development are best developed through reading and writing, we must provide the time and opportunity for students to apply their learning in context. However, if we have not determined the learning goal, do not know how it will be met, or do not allow students to attain ownership of the learning, our time will not be well spent. Figure 5.3 depicts the data in a school where learning targets are not integrated into instructional planning and delivery.

Figure 5.3 | *Example of Learning Target/Instructional Goal Data from Literacy Classroom Visits*

LEARNING TARGET/INSTRUCTIONAL GOAL
25%   Learning target/goal is posted in student-friendly language.
10%   Learning target/goal identifies demonstration of learning (performance criteria).
15%   Learning target/goal is taught and monitored across the gradual release of responsibility.
Comments: Learning targets (LTs) were not consistently posted in classrooms. In some classrooms, the learning target was posted in standard language. LTs did not typically describe performance criteria or what students would need to do. 15% of teachers were observed modeling, guiding, or assessing the LT. Students were not observed practicing or demonstrating the LT in the majority of classrooms.

In this example, the district expected teachers to use learning targets in their classrooms after they received a brief training early in the school year. The training introduced the concept of learning targets and then informed teachers of the expectation, which the principal would monitor using a walkthrough process. For several weeks after the training, the principal reported that learning targets were posted in every classroom. However, the teachers posted the targets because they were expected to do so; it was an act of compliance rather than a sign of instructional change. The brief training did not develop teachers' interest in learning targets or fully explain their purpose and importance. Nor did the district provide sustained training to guide teachers in writing or teaching effective learning targets or in teaching and assessing them across the gradual release. As a result, the practice dissipated as time elapsed.

Learning Forward's senior distinguished fellow Hayes Mizell (2010) asserts that professional learning must be both job-embedded and *sustained*. If we expect teachers to integrate new learning into their practice, we need to roll out a full implementation process that shares pertinent information, discusses a process for implementing and supporting new practices, has teachers collaborate with colleagues, and assesses progress over time (Croft, Coggshall, Dolan, Powers, & Killion, 2010).

The LCV data in Figure 5.3 indicated that most teachers in this school were not developing learning targets or posting them in their classrooms. The teachers lacked buy-in and a purpose for adopting the practice. They needed to believe that the development and use of learning targets were worth their investment of time and energy. Thus, an action plan to address this area of need requires the leader to share the purpose and rationale for using learning targets, examples of strong learning targets, and resources on how to write, teach, and assess them. In addition, teachers in this school need to see learning targets as something that will benefit students and increase their learning rather than as a requirement for district data collection. They also need to receive continual feedback on their progress.

Enhancing the LCV instrument to address the area of focus. To address the specific area of learning targets and provide ongoing professional development, you may enhance the relevant segment of the LCV instrument you use when conducting classroom visits. By paying close attention to this area during your LCVs, you can give teachers specific feedback about how well they are applying their professional learning.

To home in on the area of learning targets, you will first need to generate best-practices criteria that encompass the look-for elements. After teachers read and discuss books or articles about learning targets in PLC or staff meetings, you can collaborate with them to generate a list of characteristics of effective learning targets, establish a comprehensive school checklist, and use these elements to enhance the learning target segment of the LCV instrument (see Figure 5.4, also available online, for an example of how this may look). Then share the newly established focus and criteria with teachers and make certain that everyone understands each element listed. Determine areas where professional learning is needed and create an action plan that includes time for learning and discussion, implementation of the learning in the classroom, and reflection on the teaching experiences and student work products. Periodic visits to each classroom using the agreed-upon characteristics as enhanced LCV look-fors will identify the degree to which the new learning is being integrated into practice. Identify an LCV team to gather ongoing data as teachers refine their practices to include the elements identified in the enhanced LCV instrument.

Pattern 3: Whole-Group Instruction Does Not Prepare Students for Independent Application

Ineffective whole-group instruction may be the result of (1) an overly long lesson, (2) a nonexistent or poorly constructed learning target, (3) an attempt by the teacher to cover too much content, or (4) a lack of student interaction and engagement with teacher and peers. The lesson's ineffectiveness could stem from just one of these factors or from a combination of them. Note that this pattern can tie in to Pattern 2, as the teacher must have a goal for what he or she wishes students to learn, know, do, and show as a result of the lesson.

Figure 5.4 | *Example of an Enhanced Learning Target/ Instructional Goal Segment from the LCV Instrument*

Enhanced Literacy Classroom Visit Instrument (Check-In)		
OBSERVED METHOD OF INSTRUCTIONAL DELIVERY		
☐ **Whole-Group Lesson/Mini-Lesson**	☐ **Small-Group Lesson**	☐ **Independent Reading and Application**
LEARNING TARGET/INSTRUCTIONAL GOAL		

☐ Learning target/goal is posted and visible in the learning area.

☐ Learning target/goal is written in student-friendly, culturally respectful language.

☐ Learning target/goal is aligned to standards and student development expectations.

☐ Learning target/goal describes what students will learn by the end of the lesson.

☐ Learning target/goal identifies demonstration of learning (performance criteria).

☐ Learning target/goal is taught and monitored across the gradual release of responsibility.

☐ Students have ownership in and can explain their learning and can articulate the learning target at any point during the gradual release of responsibility.

☐ No learning target/goal is posted or observed.

If the purpose of whole-group instruction is to explicitly teach and model a learning goal that students can then practice, then the instruction must be timely, focused, and precise. The teacher must also believe that the purpose of the whole-group lesson is to set students up to learn with peers and on their own.

The data in Figure 5.5 show that the teachers in this school are tied to their whole-group methodology. Digging deeper into this area may require additional classroom visits, but based on these data, we can draw some conclusions about teachers' belief systems and methods of student engagement.

A large percentage of teachers (64 percent) were engaged in whole-group teaching, yet only half of those teachers (30 percent) were explicitly teaching and modeling the learning target, indicating that the gradual release of responsibility may not be used effectively throughout the school. The teachers understand the importance of a focused whole-group lesson, but what is the focus, and why are the teachers not modeling that focused goal? Do the learning target/instructional goal data indicate that the writing, teaching, and assessing of learning targets are established practices? Why was so much whole-group teaching observed? These data offer a great foundation for questions, but the answers to those questions may require additional rounds of LCVs focused on whole-group instruction and other elements.

Figure 5.5 | *Example of Whole-Group Explicit Instruction Data from Literacy Classroom Visits*

WHOLE-GROUP EXPLICIT INSTRUCTION		
64% Whole-Group Lesson/Mini-Lesson	16% Small-Group Lesson	20% Independent Reading and Application

80% Teacher is leading a focused mini-lesson or lesson.

30% Teacher is explicitly teaching/modeling effective skill/strategy (learning target).

70% Students are actively listening, purposefully engaged, and interacting with teacher.

10% Students are actively listening, purposefully engaged, and interacting with peers.

Whole group was being conducted in about 64% of classrooms observed (data taken from observers indicating whole group, small group, or independent reading and application on the LCV instrument).

Comments: Learning targets were posted and part of the teaching in fewer than half of the classrooms. The majority of lessons did not include explicit teaching and modeling. Most teachers were telling, explaining, and questioning to deliver the content. Students were engaged with the teacher and responding to questions by raising hands. In some classrooms, teachers used popsicle sticks to randomly call on students. In few classrooms were students asked to collaborate among themselves while teachers assessed learning.

The data also indicate that teachers are aware of the importance of student engagement and have strategies to foster teacher-student interaction. However, there was little evidence of engagement and collaboration among students. Teachers may benefit from seeing criteria identified in the look-for elements of effective whole-group instruction (see Figure 5.6, also available online; see note on p. 5) and receiving professional development in engagement strategies, along with some resources to support those strategies.

Pattern 4: Teachers Are Instructing Instead of Coaching in Small-Group Guided Practice

The purpose of small-group instruction is to give students time to practice decoding and comprehension strategies as they read a text at their instructional level and discuss their understanding with peers. During this phase of the gradual release, the teacher takes on the role of coach and selects texts that provide challenge while guiding students to collaboratively practice a skill or strategy that was taught in whole group or that will address a pre-identified need. Small groups ideally contain no more than six members and are flexible, depending on students' ongoing needs; the teacher regularly adjusts group membership using data collected from assessment, observation, and conferring. The teacher also

Figure 5.6 | *Example of an Enhanced Whole-Group Explicit Instruction Segment from the LCV Instrument*

Enhanced Literacy Classroom Visit Instrument (Check-In)		
OBSERVED METHOD OF INSTRUCTIONAL DELIVERY		
☐ **Whole-Group Lesson/Mini-Lesson**	☐ **Small-Group Lesson**	☐ **Independent Reading and Application**
WHOLE-GROUP EXPLICIT INSTRUCTION		
☐ Teacher is leading a mini-lesson or lesson.		
☐ The lesson is focused, and the learning target or goal is clear to students.		
☐ Teacher is using time effectively for age range.		
☐ Teacher activates students' prior knowledge.		
☐ Teacher sets the purpose for the lesson.		
☐ Teacher is explicitly teaching/modeling effective skill/strategy (learning target).		
☐ Teacher is explaining and assigning.		
☐ Teacher is questioning or guiding.		
☐ Teacher uses several engagement strategies to assess students' understanding.		
☐ Teacher provides guided practice before releasing students to practice on their own.		
☐ Students are actively listening, purposefully engaged, and interacting with teacher.		
☐ Students are actively listening, purposefully engaged, and interacting with peers.		
☐ Students leave whole group ready to practice the learning target both with peers and on their own.		

- Observes, assesses, and collects data about students' fluency and comprehension development as he or she listens to students read and apply strategies.
- Uses text-based and higher-order questions to promote deep, insightful discussions about the text and notes students' progress in gaining meaning from complex text.
- Makes observational notes about how students are progressing and further determines their needs. These data are used to support, reteach, extend, and plan for continuous learning.

Figure 5.7 shows data from a school whose teachers are clearly not effectively implementing these small-group practices in their classrooms.

Only 12 percent of the classroom teachers were observed engaging in small-group instruction, falling short of the general goal of dividing class time roughly evenly among whole-group, small-group, and independent instructional opportunities. Although balancing instruction across the gradual release doesn't necessarily mean that each area of instructional

Figure 5.7 | *Example of Small-Group Guided*
Practice Data from Literacy Classroom Visits

SMALL-GROUP GUIDED PRACTICE
6% Teacher is guiding students' reading, strategy application, and collaborative discussions.
2% Teacher is listening to students read individually while others read quietly.
2% Teacher is assessing strengths/needs and collecting anecdotal notes.
4% Students are reading and discussing texts at their instructional level.
6% Students are practicing the skill or strategy explicitly taught and modeled in whole group.
Small group was being conducted in about 12% of classrooms observed (data taken from observers indicating whole group, small group, or independent reading and application on the LCV instrument).
Comments: We observed few small-group sessions. In observed situations, the teacher was serving as the teacher rather than the coach or guide. However, a few teachers were coaching students in application of learning and higher-order thinking. Teachers prompted students' responses using questions. Some students read from the text and were asked to summarize. In about half of the small groups observed, students were interacting with instructional-level texts and practicing the learning target.

delivery must take up exactly one-third of the class, when one of the three segments is significantly longer or shorter than that, it indicates an issue that needs delving into. Of the 12 percent of teachers who *were* engaging in small-group instruction, only about half were serving in the role of coach. Although some students were practicing their learning, responding to questions, and engaging in discussions, teachers were not using this opportunity to observe, assess, and ask students to model learning while they recorded data.

This pattern can be connected to Patterns 2 and 3. If teachers believe that they are the impetus for learning, they will have a hard time shifting to a coaching or guidance stance. Relying too heavily on whole-group instruction deprives students of opportunities to practice and apply strategies using texts at their instructional level. Nor does whole-group instruction provide a vehicle for teachers to truly assist students as they develop their literacy skills. Similarly, if teachers do not understand or believe in the importance of releasing the ownership of learning to students, they will continue to stay in control by maintaining the teacher stance during small-group time. Finally, if teachers did not set the students up to practice together during the whole-group lesson, they will need to teach the lesson again during small-group instruction. These are all factors that may make small-group practice less effective.

Another potential contributor to this common pattern is a lack of framework, process, or routine for students to work together in small groups, with or without the teacher. This ties back to Pattern 1 and the need for rituals, routines, and procedures to support balanced literacy.

Figure 5.8 (also available online; see note on p. 5) illustrates how leaders can work with teachers to unpack the best practices for small-group guided reading and create a check-in for digging deeper into this area of literacy instruction.

Figure 5.8 | *Example of an Enhanced Small-Group Guided Practice Segment from the LCV Instrument*

Enhanced Literacy Classroom Visit Instrument (Check-In)
OBSERVED METHOD OF INSTRUCTIONAL DELIVERY
☐ **Whole-Group Lesson/Mini-Lesson**   ☐ **Small-Group Lesson**   ☐ **Independent Reading and Application**
SMALL-GROUP GUIDED PRACTICE
☐ Teacher is reteaching the whole-group content.   ☐ Teacher is guiding students' strategy application practice.   ☐ Teacher is guiding students' reading development.   ☐ Teacher is guiding students' collaborative discussions.   ☐ Teacher is listening to students read individually while others read quietly.   ☐ Teacher is assessing strengths/needs and collecting anecdotal notes.   ☐ Students are reading and discussing texts at their instructional level.   ☐ Students are practicing the skill or strategy explicitly taught and modeled in whole group.   ☐ Students are asking and answering higher-order questions with peers.   ☐ Students are close-reading short segments of complex text.   ☐ Students are answering and discussing text-dependent questions created by the teacher.   ☐ Students have a framework for discussing complex texts and ideas with or without the teacher.

Pattern 5: Students Don't Get Enough Time for Independent Reading and Application

One of the highest priorities of a balanced literacy classroom is developing students' independent reading skills. For students to become wise readers and develop the skills and strategies to maximize comprehension, they need a classroom library equipped and organized for student self-selection, a procedure to self-select texts to practice their learning, and time to develop their stamina to read for up to 30 minutes every day.

If teachers don't have a schedule to confer with students weekly or biweekly and collect data about the students' interests, application of learning, and progress as readers, then students will not continue to develop as wise readers. The teacher also needs methods of collecting, analyzing, and using data about each student's reading development. Schools with a strong literacy culture devote at least one-third of the literacy block to independent reading of self-selected texts and conferring to collect timely data. For the school whose data appear in Figure 5.9, we can see that this is not the case.

Figure 5.9 | *Example of Independent Reading and Application Data from Literacy Classroom Visits*

INDEPENDENT READING AND APPLICATION
2% Teacher is conferring one-on-one with reader.
0% Teacher is assessing development and recording data.
6% Students are reading self-selected books from a bag or bin and applying strategies learned.
2% Students are conferring with teacher about reading skills and/or demonstrating learning target.
18% Students are actively working at some other connected literacy enhancement activity.
Independent reading and application observed in 24% of classrooms (data taken from observers indicating whole group, small group, or independent reading and application on the LCV instrument).
Comments: Fewer than one-fourth of classrooms were participating in independent reading structures. Few students in each class were focused on literacy-related activities during the literacy block. Only 6% of the students were reading self-selected books independently. For the 6% who were reading self-selected books, no strategy application was noted. The majority of students were reading assigned text or doing seatwork and other activities.

Although the classrooms observed did devote some time to independent reading and application, that time was used for completing assignments from the teacher rather than engaging in authentic reading and writing experiences. This issue can be tied to Pattern 1: if teachers do not have the foundations in place for the gradual release of responsibility and for students to read and write independently, this key area cannot thrive.

This pattern may also be connected to teachers' level of commitment in shifting ownership of learning to students. Teachers in these classrooms may believe that their instruction is a priority or that their job is to deliver content rather than facilitate students' learning, resulting in whole-group instruction dominating the literacy block. The problem may also be linked to an ineffectively designed learning target (Pattern 2). Without a clear learning goal, a teacher cannot plan focused whole-group lessons to explicitly teach and model performance criteria so that students can practice and master the target in small groups and on their own.

If a lack of independent reading and application is a concern within your school, you can use the form in Figure 5.10 (also available online; see note on p. 5) to further identify and analyze specific issues that you can then address through professional learning, instructional practices, and student application. Watch **Video 5.2** to see how a team from Gaithersburg Elementary School met to conduct Literacy Classroom Visits with a particular focus on independent reading.

Figure 5.10 | *Example of an Enhanced Independent Reading and Application Segment from the LCV Instrument*

Enhanced Literacy Classroom Visit Instrument (Check-In)		
OBSERVED METHOD OF INSTRUCTIONAL DELIVERY		
☐ **Whole-Group Lesson/Mini-Lesson**	☐ **Small-Group Lesson**	☐ **Independent Reading and Application**
INDEPENDENT READING AND APPLICATION		
Classroom libraries:		
☐ Fewer than 300 texts. ☐ 300–500 texts. ☐ 500+ texts. ☐ A variety of informational text and text features. ☐ A balance of nonfiction/fiction (40%/60%). ☐ A range of reading levels (span at least four grades). ☐ Books of interest to students. ☐ Organized in multiple ways. ☐ Space is organized effectively. ☐ Books are labeled or students know about *just right* books. ☐ Books are appealing; library space is inviting. ☐ Evidence of student use _____		

STUDENTS are independently reading and responding to text:
☐ Reading self-selected books.
☐ Choosing from a variety of texts on desk or in a bag or bin.
☐ Applying strategies with independent text.
☐ Conferring with a teacher.
☐ Reading a variety of genres.
☐ Reading self-selected informational text with text features.
☐ Writing in response to reading through journals or logs.
☐ Engaging in word work.
☐ Engaging in Literacy Work Stations.
☐ Sharing what they read in groups or with partners.
☐ Reading independently with deep engagement.

The TEACHER is conferring, observing, assessing independent reading:
☐ Actively observing students in classroom.
☐ Conferring one-on-one with readers.
☐ Recording conferring data.
☐ Assessing students' fluency and/or comprehension.
☐ Noting strategy application.
☐ Providing direct instruction (individual/small group).
☐ Explaining a new Literacy Work Station.
☐ Modeling a strategy used in independent reading.
☐ Observing or providing feedback to student-led discussions.

Using Enhanced Literacy Classroom Visit Instruments

Let's review the process of the LCV Model thus far. First, you established staff buy-in to the process by sharing the LCV instrument and explaining all of its components. Then, together with a few other educators, you conducted one to three classroom visits using the LCV instrument and gathering data to better understand your school's current literacy culture. Next, you analyzed the data and discussed the patterns that emerged; for example, maybe your LCV team noted that whole-group instruction took up too much of the literacy block of instruction or that classrooms didn't allot enough time for independent reading.

Now, you are ready to refine the LCV instrument to address the patterns you identified. Select one area of focus—say, independent reading and application—and identify the look-for components to use. Our online resources (see note on p. 5) offer examples of individual templates of the enhanced look-fors for each component of the LCV instrument. You can use these templates with Google Forms or other electronic means as well as with a hard-copy system of data collection. The LCV Whole-School Instrument is an example of how to make data collection easier when using a hard-copy system. Then, begin to use the enhanced LCV instrument for the component you've identified to monitor and provide feedback about the implementation of professional learning and new resources.

Summarizing the Data Analysis

If all of the examples we've used in this chapter to illustrate the common patterns were found in a single school, deciding where to begin would be a challenge. Fortunately, it is unusual to find extreme cases of all five issues within one community. Typically, patterns arise indicating one or two fields of critical need. Addressing these areas will have a positive effect on the school's overall teaching and learning as well as its developing literacy culture. However, if your team has identified numerous areas of need, you'll need to prioritize the work. We have found that there are three high-priority elements that must be in place before you can build your continuous-progress model of literacy development:

1. A classroom environment and culture that support effective balanced literacy instruction.
2. Learning targets that are effectively written, taught, and assessed across the gradual release of responsibility.
3. Independent student reading of self-selected texts for up to 30 minutes each day.

In other words, classroom structure, management, and culture must support the work of effective literacy instruction; teachers must believe in the importance of releasing the ownership of learning to students and teach in a balanced way to ensure this shift; and students must have time to practice what we want them to learn.

Our overarching goal is to create self-directed, self-motivated critical thinkers and problem solvers who love to read. This cannot happen if we do not create the structure to develop these behaviors. If these three areas are strongly seated in the literacy culture of your classrooms, you can focus on other areas. In Chapters 6 and 7, we provide a comprehensive overview of developing professional learning plans and opportunities.

Planning for Professional Growth

6

High-quality professional learning is the foundation on which any improvement effort in education must build.

—Thomas Guskey, "Planning Professional Learning," in *Educational Leadership*

Research (Cole, 2005; Darling-Hammond & Bransford, 2005; Marzano, 2003; Reeves, 2010) shows that teacher success can be cultivated by high-quality professional learning. The key word here, of course, is *high-quality*: to be effective, professional learning must continue over time, and embedding new learning into professional practices requires ongoing support. The primary goals for professional learning are changes in educator practice and increases in student learning. Such large-scale change doesn't happen overnight; teachers need time to apply new learning in their classrooms, discuss their experiences with colleagues, and add new learning to their overall teaching practice.

Unfortunately, the current state of professional learning in the United States leaves much to be desired. A study led by Linda Darling-Hammond (Darling-Hammond, Chung Wei, Andree, & Richardson, 2009) discovered that more than 90 percent of professional development provided for teachers each year was in the form of traditional "one-and-done" workshops, with little or no follow-up. Research (Bush, 1984; Yoon, Duncan, Lee, Scarloss, & Shapley, 2007) shows that these brief learning experiences often don't change teacher practice and have no effect on student achievement, yet this approach is still prevalent in many settings. Not only is the United States dated in its practices, but recent studies (Wei, Darling-Hammond, & Adamson, 2010) even suggest that we have moved *backward* in our efforts to provide teachers with the kind of ongoing, intensive professional learning that has been shown to have a substantial effect on student learning. Since 2008, budget cuts have resulted in teachers nationwide receiving fewer and fewer opportunities to engage in sustained professional learning opportunities. They are also half as likely as teachers were in 2000 to report collaborative efforts in their schools.

The good news is that the LCV Model is seated in the research-supported practices necessary to support the types of changes in teacher practice that truly result in student growth.

A Professional Learning Design for Literacy

Professional learning is more than just attending periodic workshops or conferences. It requires an investment in time, careful planning by a leadership team, and ongoing progress monitoring and data conversations to ensure that it is changing practice and effecting student growth (Gulamhussein, 2013).

A starting point in designing effective professional learning for educators is the development of a literacy plan for the school that identifies strengths and needs, sets appropriate goals, lists professional learning activities, and outlines a projected time line complete with dates and people responsible for each actionable item.

When creating a plan for professional learning, leaders must consider multiple factors. The initial step is to determine the intended outcome, which can be drawn from analysis of both students' and teachers' learning needs. Adult learners are best able to apply their learning when they integrate new processes into their instruction and have time to reflect on their experiences with colleagues. Reviewing student work related to the newly implemented instructional practices can enrich the peer conversations. Finally, ongoing feedback and coaching from instructional leaders can enhance the entire experience. Figure 6.1 depicts a model of effective professional learning that incorporates these important factors.

This professional learning design is devised to encourage gradual release of responsibility for professional learning to the staff. In using the model, teachers acquire new content, study and discuss it, apply it, and make revisions until the learning becomes integrated into the school's culture. Teachers are supported as they implement the new learning in their classrooms through peer coaching and mentoring by the principal. Ongoing data are collected by the principal, coach, or other designated instructional leader or team and discussed with teachers to ensure that the professional learning is timely and aligned to teacher and student needs.

Figure 6.1 | *A Professional Learning Design Using the LCV Model*

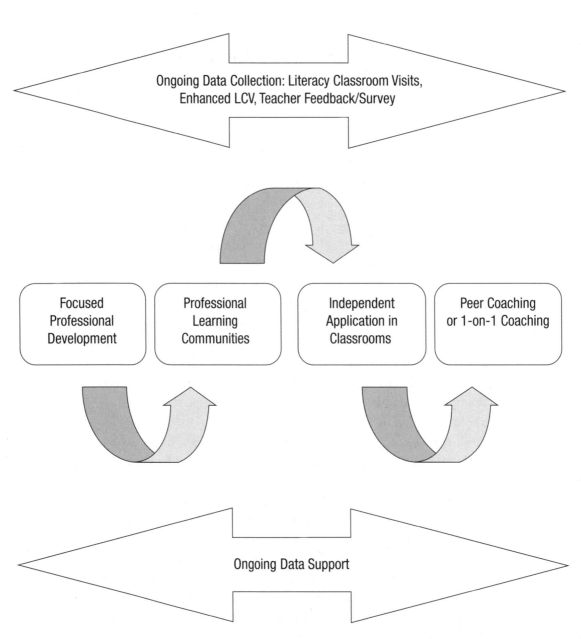

Where to Begin?

The LCV Model focuses on a school's developing culture of literacy and on instructional practices that foster student learning in reading, critical thinking, and problem solving. We have found that many schools' professional learning needs tend to fall into one of the following five categories:

1. Understanding balanced literacy instruction and developing *a culture of literacy* in a district, school, or classroom.
2. Fostering deeper understanding, development, and use of *learning targets* to guide instruction *across the gradual release of responsibility.*
3. Expanding teachers' capacity to explicitly teach and model learning through *whole-group interactive instruction.*
4. Practicing and applying whole-group learning in *small-group guided instruction and student collaboration.*
5. Culminating the gradual release model of instruction by increasing teachers' knowledge, understanding, and use of *independent reading and application of learning.*

What if your leadership team identifies multiple areas of need? Some teams may need a great deal of training in each area, while others may need only a short review of some aspects and much deeper, long-term work in other areas. **Video 6.1** shows a group of principals at a training wondering where to begin with multiple areas of need.

Deciding where to start depends on the needs of your staff as identified by the LCV data, your observations, and teacher input. We have found that teams benefit by choosing one of three possible starting points:

1. If the data reveal inconsistencies in fostering and supporting a literacy environment and culture, it is important to address this area first. The classroom environment, library, rituals and routines, and literacy opportunities provided for students create the foundational structures to support literacy instruction.
2. If teachers have a traditional approach to teaching reading with very little understanding of balanced literacy instruction and the gradual release of responsibility, professional learning must help teachers learn how to develop clear instructional goals and teach them across the gradual release. This professional learning begins with developing effective learning targets and focusing on responsive, interactive whole-group instruction.

3. If teachers have a basic understanding of balanced literacy and the gradual release of responsibility, a focus on independent reading and data collection through conferring will provide the opportunity to cultivate reading behaviors and collect formative data useful in differentiating instruction and planning small-group instruction.

Examples of Effective Professional Learning

The power of effective professional learning comes from the trust, communication, and leadership that support and sustain it. In the two examples that follow, leaders teamed with teachers to develop professional learning that led to significant growth for educators—which, in turn, positively affected student achievement.

Example 1: A Focus on Independent Reading

Clearview Elementary

Clearview Elementary is a diverse K–5 suburban school that serves 750 students, 78 percent of whom receive subsidized lunches and about 35 percent of whom have limited English proficiency. At Clearview, the LCV data indicated that students were not reading self-selected texts during the school day, and few students were reading at home daily. Recognizing the importance of daily reading of self-selected texts, the staff embarked on a three-year plan to enhance independent reading throughout the school. The Clearview leadership team started by attending a conference to build foundational knowledge about independent reading and brought back ideas, tools, and resources to help them begin to change practice and develop their reading culture. During the first year of the plan, staff focused on establishing an independent reading culture in every classroom, throughout the school, and even at home. Year 2 of the long-range plan focused on developing and deepening teachers' knowledge, understanding, and use of conferring practices. Year 3 provided professional learning on teaching students to respond to text through writing and on incorporating student-led discussions. Throughout the three years, professional learning and discussions also focused on developing and teaching learning targets across the gradual release to give students ownership of their literacy journey.

Within two years, students were keeping a variety of books and supportive resources in an individual book bin. The majority of students were independently reading books of their choice, and teachers in most classrooms were observed conferring with students and collecting data. Informational text made up about 30 percent of the choice material that students were reading, compared with about 1 percent during the initial classroom visits. Students felt motivated to read their self-selected texts and were able to maintain engagement for 30 minutes or more.

As reported by the principal and reading specialist and supported by LCV data, Clearview teachers have directly applied their new methods to everyday routines, and their student data inform them that their teaching practices are more effective. Data further indicate that the more clearly the leadership team articulated the professional learning targets and described the activities for the entire school year, the better the teachers implemented the new teaching strategies and skills—which also meant an increase in student reading success.

The teachers at Clearview embraced the belief that professional learning is most effective when it is ongoing and aligned to and integrated into their daily teaching practices. Therefore, they set up a plan to study skills and strategies important to key areas of content, tried them out in the classroom, discussed their experiences with colleagues, made revisions based on new learning, and repeated the process until they attained mastery. Their three-year plan aligned with the criteria for effective professional development programs as described in the Standards for Professional Learning (Learning Forward, 2011): it incorporated relevant research; demonstration of new knowledge, skills, and strategies; opportunities for practice and self-reflection; feedback from leaders and peers; and follow-up support to help teachers hone newly acquired skills. When professional development merely describes a skill to teachers, only 10 percent can transfer it to their practice; however, when teachers discuss their changing practices and are coached through implementation, 95 percent can transfer the skill (Bush, 1984; Truesdale, 2003). Therefore, to continue building teachers' foundational knowledge, Clearview used a variety of contexts to extend their learning and application of effective practices related to independent reading. The following sections take a closer look at Clearview's process.

Professional Reading

First, PLC teams selected topics for professional reading and study. Professional reading, while often overlooked, encourages teachers to investigate issues and problems that have risen in their own teaching experience and search for solutions that will enhance their knowledge and skill base (Rock & Levin, 2002). Clearview educators read multiple texts to learn about specific aspects of independent reading instruction and student learning, including readings from *Creating Lifelong Readers Through Independent Reading* (Moss & Young, 2010) and *No More Independent Reading Without Support* (Miller & Moss, 2013).

Reading the views of multiple authors stimulates discussion and models the work required in English language arts standards, while deeper review of the text enhances teachers' understanding. Discussing their reading with peers also helps teachers apply new knowledge in their classrooms.

PLC Discussions

Clearview teachers met in grade-level PLC teams, vertical teams, and other groupings throughout the year—depending on the work and purpose for each professional learning discussion—to analyze, problem-solve, and reflect on shared examples of actual teaching and instructional planning related to independent reading.

Rather than just reading and talking about books, teachers immersed themselves deeply in the content by bringing the experiences from the texts into their classrooms. For example, after teachers read Chapter 2 of *Creating Lifelong Readers Through Independent Reading* (Moss & Young, 2010), they took an inventory of their classroom libraries using the checklist provided in the book and chose to participate in one of two PLC activities.

PLC Activity A. Moss and Young (2010) assert that students' preferences for certain kinds of books should not only be honored but also form an important basis for classroom library selection. Accordingly,

Clearview teachers participating in this activity administered the authors' Reading Interest Survey (on page 57 of their book) to students. After reviewing the data from the survey, each teacher selected three students from his or her classroom: an above-grade-level reader, an on-grade-level reader, and a below-grade-level reader. Then they matched each student's interests to "just right" books from their classroom collections and brought examples to share with their PLC and discuss how students reacted to this approach, answering the following questions:

- Did your students enjoy reading these books?
- What process did you use to match texts with students' interests?
- Were you able to accommodate all students' needs?

PLC Activity B. Moss and Young (2010) tell us that "in order to become successful readers, students need exposure to a variety of genres" (pp. 54–55). Clearview teachers participating in this activity went into *one* classroom library and determined which genres were represented in the collection. They then identified the Developmental Reading Assessment level (or Lexile level) of the nonfiction books to determine whether all students had a variety of genres to choose from. Then, from their own classroom libraries, teachers selected a nonfiction genre that all students would explore reading independently over the next couple of weeks. The teachers reported their students' experience to their PLC group, discussing the following questions:

- Were all students able to find a book within that particular genre?
- What focus lessons did you need to teach to make the text more accessible for students and give them the background knowledge they needed to be successful?
- Did students enjoy reading this genre?

At Clearview, PLC discussions about texts grew richer and more focused on application as teachers engaged in this collegial work throughout the year. Educators' interactions broadened their perspectives and enhanced their understanding of independent reading.

Independent Application and Coaching

Armed with strong foundational knowledge about independent reading acquired from workshops, whole-group presentations, and other periodic professional learning experiences, teachers at Clearview planned lessons based on their new learning and received coaching from Laura, a master educator and reading specialist. Combining self-reflection and coaching before, during, and after a lesson provided timely feedback to teachers about their implementation of newly learned instructional skills. As numerous studies (Batt, 2010; Knight, 2007; Knight & Cornett, 2009; Showers, 1984; Slinger, 2004; Stephens et al., 2007) have shown, coaching is an effective way to change teacher practice and improve student learning. Even experienced teachers struggle with new instructional techniques in the beginning and benefit from collegial conversations and coaching (Ermeling, 2010; Joyce & Showers, 1982).

We wanted a strong independent reading program but had never really given thought to the essential components to make it happen. The Literacy Classroom Visit Model gave us a lens through which we could look to see if independent reading was truly happening in our classrooms and to address needs through professional learning.

Simply observing students reading in classrooms was not enough. When we first used the tool in 34 classrooms, we felt good about the number of students engaged in reading self-selected texts and the variety of genres they were reading but could see that students were not really talking about their books. We also noticed that our staff needed professional development around conferring with students to establish reading goals and record student progress.

The LCV Model made it easy for us to identify schoolwide professional development needs. Our most recent collection of data revealed that our teachers have a stronger understanding of independent reading, which leads us to believe our professional development efforts over the past two years have been effective.

Laura Hankins, Reading Specialist

Using the LCV Instrument to Monitor Implementation of Professional Learning

In Chapter 5, we described common patterns that may emerge from the initial series of classroom visits. Then we provided an example of an enhanced Literacy Classroom Visit instrument that can be used to check in on the professional learning efforts being implemented throughout the school. As leaders move through the LCV process, they may wish to develop their own enhanced instruments to focus their classroom visits more closely on the work being done in their school or district. Using our examples, leaders can discuss the look-fors aligned to their current professional learning and collect specific data to inform the implementation and integration of new learning into instructional practice.

The principal and the literacy leadership team at Clearview used the independent reading and application enhanced Literacy Classroom Visit instrument (see Figure 5.10) as they conducted classroom visits three times during each of the three years in their long-term improvement plan. The data yielded by the enhanced LCV instrument enabled Clearview staff to determine the next steps for professional learning.

This kind of ongoing approach divides professional development into manageable and measurable portions of learning across a long-range trajectory. Ongoing data during the first year indicated that although students were reading more in self-selected, "just right" texts and had increased stamina for independent reading, the teachers were not consistently conferring with students or collecting data about reading development. LCV data showed that teachers were developing at different rates and had differing needs. The coach was able to differentiate through targeted training, demonstration, coaching, and PLC study to build capacity in all teachers. By the end of the second year, data indicated that most teachers were successfully integrating conferring into their instructional practices. The leadership team believed that part of the initiative's success could be attributed to the fact that every teacher knew the look-fors on the LCV instrument that were tailored to identify their level of implementation.

As an added benefit of using the LCV Model at Clearview, teachers found value in being part of the LCV team. They appreciated the collegial conversations they had as they analyzed whole-school data and the knowledge they gained from other members of the team. By being on an LCV team, they felt more effective as educators.

Evidence collected from the LCV as well as student achievement data suggested that the professional learning at Clearview had led to fundamental changes to instruction along with improvements in student performance. Although it is still early to claim long-term effects, professional learning is clearly ongoing, and teachers' appetite to continue this process is strong—a good thing, since continued collaboration and focus are needed to maintain the positive changes in teaching practice and student performance.

Formative classroom visits help educators engage one another in confronting and assimilating research and theory. They help teachers to regularly evaluate their own practices in a safe culture characterized by mutual assistance and sustained through coaching and collaborative problem solving around specific issues of practice (Moss & Brookhart, 2015). Implementing the LCV Model at Clearview has helped teachers hone their craft while fostering the learning of everyone in the school.

Example 2: Balanced Literacy and the Gradual Release of Responsibility

McHenry Elementary

McHenry Elementary School is a K–5 school in a large urban area. The principal has been at the school for more than 20 years, as have many staff members. Data from a series of Literacy Classroom Visits and a teacher survey showed that most of the classrooms had libraries, rituals and routines, and environments that supported the gradual release of balanced literacy instruction. Teachers had also engaged in professional learning in developing learning targets, but the instruction to support the learning targets was not gradually released to students in small-group situations or applied while they were reading their chosen texts.

Data indicated that teachers were doing the heavy lifting in the classroom and not fully releasing responsibility to students. Whole-group instruction was the main method of instructional delivery, followed by student application using worksheets. Many teachers were tied to the basal text and its resources. Small groups primarily worked on teacher-generated student projects rather than engaging in guided discussion about texts.

During the data analysis with the leadership team, it became clear that professional learning needed to center on understanding the Balanced Literacy Gradual Release Model of Reading Instruction and strengthening teaching across the gradual release of responsibility to transfer the ownership of learning to the students.

The first year was structured according to the Professional Learning Design Using the LCV Model (see Figure 6.1). Two full-day and two half-day workshops were offered across the year, with weekly PLC meetings between workshops to continue the discussion and implementation of learning. The first full-day workshop was offered in August, followed by a half-day in early November. The second full-day workshop occurred in January and was followed by a half-day in March. These workshops provided the structure for foundational content learning. The first workshop focused on balanced literacy and the gradual release of responsibility, specifically using the learning target as the focus of turning ownership of learning over to students. Teachers reviewed the six components of reading identified by the National Reading Panel (National Institute of Child Health and Human Development, 2000) and the National Early Literacy Panel (2008)—oral language development, phonemic awareness, phonics, fluency, vocabulary, and comprehension development—as well as the essential elements of whole-group, small-group, and independent reading instruction. They learned how to better deliver explicit instruction and model a goal or strategy in whole group to set students up to practice it in small group and during their 30 minutes of independent reading. The second workshop focused on moving the learning taught and modeled in whole group to small groups of students. Teachers were introduced to frameworks that would support students' discussion of difficult text and ideas and help manage student group behaviors. Teachers also learned how to use data to group students and how to choose appropriate texts based on students' interest, abilities, and experiences.

Weekly PLC meetings supported and extended this learning by using readings, videos, data, and examples of focused learning targets with accompanying student work to generate collaborative conversations and planning. A reading specialist collaborated

Continued

with the principal to conduct ongoing Literacy Classroom Visits, and the LCV instrument was modified to enhance the area of focus and help the LCV team identify how well new learning was being implemented.

PLC Discussions

Between the two whole-group workshops, PLCs used checklists in peer teams, which consisted of pairs or triads from each PLC team, to visit classrooms and discuss how they were set up to support the Balanced Literacy Gradual Release Model of Reading Instruction. The principal and reading specialist shared LCV data, noting that some teachers needed to focus on whole-group instruction, while others were ready to move on to enhancing their small-group practices. With the support of the reading specialist, PLC content was differentiated to meet teachers' diverse needs.

The school decided to take a peer-supported approach to its PLC work. Grade-level teams chose from two study foci: whole group or small group. Teachers selected and read articles to support their learning but primarily learned from demonstration lessons, viewing and discussing videos that depicted instruction and analysis of learning targets and examples of the resulting student work. Teams agreed on the criteria for enhancing the LCV instrument, so that the principal and peers from PLC groups could check in periodically and share which areas were improving. The fact that peers participated in classroom visits increased the collegiality of the LCV data analysis.

All teachers discussed examples of development and progress identified by the LCV data, and the reading specialist shared research and ideas for addressing areas of need. The ongoing learning that resulted was timely and relevant, as it responded to the current learning needs and goals of the PLC members.

PLC Group A: Whole-group focus. Teams in this PLC group discussed video examples of effective whole-group instruction, comparing the examples with their own current practice. Teachers shared their learning targets, videotaped their explicit instruction and modeling of the targets, and discussed with peers specific segments they selected from their videos that informed their group of the practices that were developing in their instruction. Teachers reviewed student work from small group and independent application, determined the percentage of students who were able to master the learning, and talked about how they could modify instruction or expectations to ensure that at least 80 percent of their students were consistently successful.

As the year progressed, teachers who were successfully transferring whole-group learning to small groups provided demonstration lessons for their peers. After the first semester of learning, whole-group instruction observed using the LCV instrument shifted from being noted 90 percent of the instructional time to 55 percent, providing evidence of the shift from whole-group-dominated instruction to increased small-group and independent practices. The teacher survey and conversations indicated that their efforts were working to shorten whole-group lessons, focus them around explicit instruction of the learning target, and provide direction for students in what to practice and apply during small group and independent reading.

PLC Group B: Small-group focus. Within the PLC focusing on small group, there was more differentiation. Two of the three teams chose to focus on how to use data to group students and select appropriate text. They also wanted to learn about coaching students in applying the learning target when reading, discussing, and using texts. Members of the third team felt that they had these small-group instructional practices in place and instead decided to develop a classroom management system and a small-group protocol for students to follow. They believed that many of their students could participate in student-led groups to extend their learning from the content taught by the teacher-guided groups.

Teachers chose partners with whom to conduct monthly classroom visits, during which they would observe the implementation of their learning. These peer observations, coupled with the broader data from the LCVs, cultivated rich, instructionally focused conversations.

The LCV and other data launched conversations about what the learning focus would be for the next workshop day. Teachers wanted to continue to work on their areas of focus but also wanted to share their learning and experiences with one another.

Professional Growth at McHenry

In the spring, each PLC team prepared a 30-minute session to share at weekly PLC meetings, highlighting their progress and showing how team members were changing the teaching and learning in their classrooms as a result of this professional learning experience. The gradual release of responsibility successfully shifted ownership for professional learning to the teachers themselves, who took on leadership roles for their colleagues.

By spring, teachers were also comfortable with the LCV process. Data indicated a critical change in the classroom environment and culture as well as growth in the movement of learning across the gradual release, highlighting a shift in the kinds of student work teachers were supporting in small groups and during independent application. Teachers were developing strong lesson plans that outlined the explicit instruction necessary to support small-group practice leading to mastery, and students were taking more responsibility for their learning. These data, along with teacher input and principal observations, were used to create the following year's professional learning plan.

Evaluating Professional Learning and Creating Lasting Change

Professional learning can have a powerful effect on teachers' knowledge and skills and on students' learning if it is ongoing, sustainable, focused on important content, embedded in the work of PLCs that support continual improvement in teachers' practice, and monitored throughout the implementation (Cole, 2012). Studies (Banilower, 2002; Yoon et al., 2007) show that effective professional development programs require anywhere from 50 to 80 hours of instruction, practice, and coaching before teachers arrive at mastery.

Despite our knowledge about what constitutes effective professional development, many districts and schools are not able to quantify the time and money they spend on long-range professional development or measure the success of that investment over time because they do not have tools to systematically evaluate it.

An effective professional development plan incorporates an examination of authentic classroom practices and the effect of professional learning on teacher practices and student learning. Evaluation of the plan must be an ongoing process starting in the earliest stages of program planning and continuing beyond the end of the program. The LCV Model is an effective way to provide leaders with data on professional development's effect on teaching practices. Expectations increase from simply grasping or demonstrating "best practices" to continuously documenting professional growth through up-to-the-minute evidence (Moss &

Brookhart, 2015). By embedding the LCV Model in a school's or district's professional learning plan, leaders will have data that help teachers hone their skills as they address the lasting changes needed to improve the literacy culture within their schools.

Whole-School Involvement Across All Content Areas

7

If students are to succeed in the content areas, teachers will need to demystify the reading and writing that go on there.

—Rafael Heller and Cynthia L. Greenleaf,
Literacy Instruction in the Content Areas

Although students are learning to read and reading to learn continuously across all grade levels and content areas, many educators erroneously consider the development of reading to be the responsibility of elementary school teachers (Houck & Ross, 2012). However, the Common Core State Standards have heightened the importance of having secondary-level students regularly engage with complex literary and informational texts and use evidence from these texts to support learning. Actively reading, discussing, and writing about these texts builds background knowledge and helps develop a comprehensive knowledge of core content (Evers, 2011).

Teachers have a crucial role in helping students reach deeper levels of comprehension and discussion of their challenging content-area texts (Bransford, Brown, & Cocking, 2000). Studies across decades (Heller & Greenleaf, 2007; Vacca, Vacca, & Mraz, 2013) conclude that content-area teachers are best equipped to support students in learning to read the texts and materials for specific content areas because they are familiar with the patterns and structures in those texts and the strategies required for comprehension. However, researchers (Wade & Moje, 2000) also note that very little reading and writing happens in most content classrooms. Instead of requiring students to read primary-source documents, scientific papers, and historic documents, as required in the Common Core standards, the vast majority of content-area teachers assign only brief readings (mainly from textbooks) and short, formulaic writing assignments (Heller & Greenleaf, 2007).

Teachers need ongoing professional learning and support to understand how to teach students to read the texts they are using and how to model strategies to support students in understanding complex texts. Yet they rarely receive such support (Sturtevant, 2003). As a start, Kosanovich and colleagues (2010) offer five research-based recommendations that content-area teachers can use to help students understand and discuss complex texts:

1. Provide explicit instruction and supportive practice to help students apply effective comprehension strategies while reading.
2. Increase opportunities for text-based peer discussion of reading content.
3. Set high standards for the texts used in content classes as well as the teaching of how to read and comprehend them.
4. Increase students' engagement in reading by providing choices of interesting texts and supportive instruction.
5. Teach the essential prior knowledge that supports text comprehension.

Districts that identify their teachers' areas of need can use these recommendations to design instruction to support growth and change. The Literacy Visit in the Content Classroom (LVCC) instrument (see Figure 7.1, also available online; see note on p. 5) lists the look-fors in identifying classroom practices that support the development of content-area literacy.

Promoting Teacher Buy-In, Engagement, and Active Involvement

As we discussed in Chapter 3, leaders can cultivate greater participation in professional learning when they understand their teachers' needs, when the learning builds on existing practices, and when leaders are included in the process. By using the LVCC Model to collect data during content classroom visits, you can begin to develop teacher buy-in to this process.

Figure 7.1 | *Literacy Visit in the Content Classroom Instrument*

Teacher/Grade_____ Date/Time _____ Observer _____

Classroom Environment and Culture	Notes:
☐ Classroom environment and instruction support the gradual release of responsibility. ☐ Evidence of content-supportive reading, writing, speaking, and listening activities is visible and displayed. ☐ Classroom library includes a variety of texts and resources, including academic articles, websites, essays, electronic media, visuals, and lab experiences that further support reading comprehension. ☐ Content-specific vocabulary and strategies are displayed to enhance student understanding. ☐ Differentiation strategies indicate scaffolding/extension of content, process, product, and environment.	
Content/Subject Area Observed	
☐ Mathematics ☐ Science ☐ Other ☐ Language Arts ☐ Social Studies	
Learning Target/Instructional Goal	
☐ Learning target/goal is posted in student-friendly language. ☐ Learning target/goal identifies demonstration of learning (performance criteria). ☐ Learning target/goal is taught and monitored across the gradual release of responsibility.	
Observed Method of Instructional Delivery	
☐ Whole-group lesson ☐ Small-group lesson ☐ Independent application	
Whole-Group Explicit Instruction	
☐ Teacher is leading a focused mini-lesson or lesson using time effectively for age range. ☐ Teacher explicitly teaches, models, and provides supportive practice of effective comprehension strategies. ☐ Students are actively listening, purposefully engaged, and interacting with teacher and peers. ☐ Teacher provides appropriate support for all students to access, engage with, and comprehend text.	

Small-Group Guided Practice	
☐ Teacher is guiding students' application of the learning target modeled in whole group. ☐ Teacher offers choice in differentiated texts to support peer discussions and apply strategic thinking. ☐ Teacher is guiding students toward student-led (self-managing) collaborative discussion groups. ☐ Teacher is observing/assessing strengths/needs and collecting anecdotal notes. ☐ Students are practicing the skill or strategy explicitly taught and modeled in whole group. ☐ Students are reading and discussing texts at their level. ☐ Students are engaged in reflective conversations to develop critical thinking and questioning skills.	
Independent Reading and Application	
☐ Teacher is conferring with students about their work: assessing development and recording data. ☐ Teacher has identified and is supporting students in need of reteaching or extension. ☐ Students are reading texts made accessible through teacher instruction or scaffolding. ☐ Students are reading self-selected texts to support or extend their learning. ☐ Students are applying or working to demonstrate the learning target or goal. ☐ Students are writing or responding in some way to texts and ideas. ☐ Students are extending content knowledge through real-life application or experiences.	
Student Interaction and Understanding	
☐ Students know what they are supposed to learn and demonstrate. ☐ Students have an opportunity to talk with peers about their reading and learning. ☐ Students are able to read and understand the texts on their own. ☐ N/A (Student not available for questions).	
Comments/Feedback/Possible Prompts for Peer Discussions (PLCs)	

Source: © 2015 by Bonnie D. Houck, EdD, and Sandi Novak. Used with permission.

Despite years of research (Lesley, 2004) supporting the need for literacy in content instruction, resistance persists, owing to teachers' beliefs about their roles and responsibilities as well as their lack of preparation as literacy teachers (Cantrell, Burns, & Callaway, 2009). Therefore, in addition to using LVCC data, it is important to survey teachers about their overall beliefs about and understandings of content-area literacy instruction and to give them time to review and discuss the data patterns that become apparent through the process.

It is also essential that content teachers have input in the design and decision making around the content and process of their professional learning and PLC study. They have the greatest understanding of the texts used, the critical thinking and strategies required to access learning from those texts, and the best means to extend the learning from the texts.

Components of the Literacy Visit in the Content Classroom Instrument

A school or district that wants to include all teachers in its professional learning plan can choose to use the Literacy Classroom Visit instrument with the Literacy Visit in the Content Classroom instrument or use the LVCC instrument alone as a starting point for gathering data. Like the LCV instrument, the LVCC instrument serves as a way to collect a wealth of data and evidence from every classroom, focusing on the six key areas of effective literacy instruction: classroom environment and culture, learning target/instructional goal, whole-group explicit instruction, small-group guided practice, independent reading and application, and student interaction and understanding.

However, the LVCC instrument's primary focus is on how instruction uses reading and writing to support students' ownership of learning through the teachers' ability to gradually release and differentiate instruction. It also identifies the specific supportive practices employed by the teacher to ensure that students are continuously increasing their ability to read and comprehend complex texts and use this knowledge to deepen their learning of content-area principles. The following sections examine each of the six components of the LVCC instrument through the lens of one school district's experience.

Classroom Environment and Culture

The Classroom Environment and Culture section of the instrument collects observational data to determine how well the classroom climate and overall instruction foster literacy and the gradual release of responsibility. All classrooms need to provide texts and resources that promote student engagement in reading, writing, listening, and speaking. Whereas language arts teachers need a strong classroom library with a balance of fiction and informational texts, content teachers need a collection of texts that include articles, primary-source documents, essays, and other resources that support and extend the content. Students also need access to electronic resources to read online and to obtain and evaluate current information.

Hancock School District's initial classroom environment and culture data (see Figure 7.2) indicated that only in a few classrooms was the responsibility for learning shifting from teachers to students. Because seeing these data can be overwhelming for teachers and dampen enthusiasm for the process, leaders analyzed and summarized these data to determine the strengths and needs of Hancock's classrooms.

Figure 7.2 | *Hancock's Classroom Environment and Culture Data*

Classroom Environment and Culture	
38%	Classroom environment and instruction support the gradual release of responsibility.
28%	Evidence of content-supportive reading, writing, speaking, and listening activities is visible and displayed.
24%	Classroom library includes a variety of texts and resources, including academic articles, websites, essays, electronic media, visuals, and lab experiences that further support reading comprehension.
42%	Content-specific vocabulary and strategies are displayed to enhance student understanding.
28%	Differentiation strategies indicate scaffolding/extension of content, process, product, and environment.

The LVCC data informed leaders that libraries in content classrooms needed updated resources and organization. Teachers needed to understand how to structure their classrooms to support greater student collaboration and independence. Finding areas for moving from whole-group to small-group settings was especially challenging in secondary classrooms, as many buildings were designed prior to national acceptance of the need to differentiate and move beyond a lecture-delivery model.

In discussing the summary of the analyzed data, teachers considered ways to accommodate students' learning preferences that required knowledge of their students, common sense, and an understanding of the theory and research of education (Tomlinson, 2014). They visualized and studied approaches to teaching that advocated active planning for student differences in classrooms and tried to organize their classrooms to respond well to variations in student readiness, interest, or learning profile (Tomlinson & Allan, 2000).

After reviewing the LVCC data and the teacher survey results, Hancock teachers realized that their content texts also had many levels of complexity that required background knowledge and understanding of key concepts and vocabulary. The addition of visual prompts and resources would support students in developing content-specific vocabulary and strategies.

Overall, discussing the data related to this section of the instrument afforded teachers the opportunity to reflect on possible changes to make to their learning environments and new resources to offer students to ensure full access to the kinds of reading, writing, and conversation necessary to develop students' capacity to read, comprehend, discuss, and use content-area texts.

Content/Subject Area and Learning Target/Instructional Goal

For these two sections of the LVCC instrument, observers note the content area and the method of instructional delivery in the classroom they are visiting—usually just one method, since visits last only three to five minutes—as well as evidence of the learning target being taught across the gradual release of responsibility.

At Hancock, data were collected in all content areas: mathematics, language arts, science, social studies, and other (e.g., health and technology) (see Figure 7.3). In the classrooms visited, whole-group instruction dominated the instructional delivery method; only in one classroom did students engage with peers in small groups. These data patterns persisted across multiple LVCC cycles at Hancock.

Teachers should use learning targets to guide the gradual release of responsibility in the classroom, and observers should be able to see evidence of instruction supporting this learning target at any point during a lesson. Yet at Hancock, although nearly two-thirds of the classrooms

Figure 7.3 | *Hancock's Content-Area and Learning Target/Instructional Goal Data*

Content/Subject Area Observed		
22% Mathematics	18% Science	14% Other
24% Language Arts	22% Social Studies	

Learning Target/Instructional Goal
68% Learning target/goal is posted in student-friendly language.
48% Learning target/goal identifies demonstration of learning (performance criteria).
28% Learning target/goal is taught and monitored across the gradual release of responsibility.

Observed Method of Instructional Delivery		
82% Whole-group lesson	2% Small-group lesson	16% Independent application

observed had posted learning targets, teachers in only about half of those classrooms were integrating them into instruction. Because the majority of teachers were delivering whole-group instruction, opportunities to observe the gradual release through practice in small groups and application by individual students were limited. Leaders decided to enhance this section of the LVCC instrument and schedule future classroom visits as they developed a plan for professional learning.

Whole-Group Explicit Instruction

During this mode of instructional delivery, the teacher uses the learning target or instructional goal to guide explicit instruction and modeling of performance criteria. The goal of whole group is to set students up to successfully work on the learning target with peers and to be able to apply it on their own while reading, writing, and thinking. It is important that the time used for whole group is aligned to students' age range and provides them with ample opportunities to respond to learning through interaction with peers and the teacher. The teacher can use responsive engagement techniques that connect to students' interests and cultural and linguistic needs. These interactions should validate, build, affirm, and bridge the learning across current and previous instructional goals (Hollie, 2011).

Hancock's whole-group instructional data (see Figure 7.4) showed teachers that they needed to model to students how to apply the learning target while reading content-area texts. Students needed their content teachers to show them how to read the texts, unpack the knowledge, and note important evidence that would contribute to their knowledge base. Hancock teachers appeared to be concentrating too much on delivering content; they needed support in making the shift to teaching students how to learn from the content themselves.

Figure 7.4 | *Hancock's Whole-Group Explicit Instruction Data*

Whole-Group Explicit Instruction	
22%	Teacher is leading a focused mini-lesson or lesson using time effectively for age range.
26%	Teacher explicitly teaches, models, and provides supportive practice of effective comprehension strategies.
68%	Students are actively listening, purposefully engaged, and interacting with teacher and peers.
32%	Teacher provides appropriate support for all students to access, engage with, and comprehend text.

Hancock teachers also needed to select strong texts for modeling and approaches to differentiate using a variety of texts to meet students' varying needs. They needed to be able to identify specific strategies that would support access to the texts and ideas being taught while explicitly modeling to students how to understand the vocabulary they needed to fully comprehend the reading.

Small-Group Guided Practice

Small-group guided practice is an important part of the gradual release of literacy instruction because it gives students time to practice new learning with peers (with or without teacher support), make connections to previous learning, and attain new levels of mastery. Teachers can guide students' application of the learning target by prompting, questioning, or leading students in tasks while monitoring their needs for differentiation through additional support or extension. Teachers can also create collaborative structures that enable students to problem-solve while they discuss their developing ideas with peers. Productive group work allows students to immerse themselves in the learning and percolate their ideas. During this time, teachers observe, listen, make notes, and reflect on how their students learn and how well their instruction meets the needs of their students.

Hancock leaders observed virtually no small-group activity during their classroom visits across several observation cycles. The very lack of data provided vital information about teachers' beliefs and practices and pointed to an important focus for professional learning. Leaders decided to schedule a round of visits to specifically look for small-group practices, first informing teachers of the days they would be visiting and asking them to consider providing small-group opportunities for students during those times.

Independent Reading and Application

The gradual release of responsibility culminates when students synthesize information, integrate new ideas with prior knowledge, and make the learning their own. Independent reading is a time when students make decisions about their own knowledge and provides an excellent opportunity for teachers to observe and talk to students about the process. In Hancock School District, students were observed in this mode of instructional delivery in fewer than 20 percent of classrooms. However, in those classrooms, two-thirds of the students were applying and practicing their learning through activities that required reading and writing (see Figure 7.5).

Figure 7.5 | *Hancock's Independent Reading and Application Data*

Independent Reading and Application	
12%	Teacher is conferring with students about their work: assessing development and recording data.
36%	Teacher has identified and is supporting students in need of reteaching or extension.
24%	Students are reading texts made accessible through teacher instruction or scaffolding.
8%	Students are reading self-selected texts to support or extend their learning.
24%	Students are applying or working to demonstrate the learning target or goal.
68%	Students are writing or responding in some way to texts and ideas.
16%	Students are extending content knowledge through real-life application or experiences.
Data derived from the 16% of classrooms that were observed teaching independent application during the LVCC.	

In reviewing all of Hancock's initial data, it was clear that mastering the gradual release was an important starting point for professional learning: teachers would need to explore how to release responsibility for learning using all modes of instruction. They also needed to be able to differentiate texts for student choice to increase motivation and ownership. The data also showed some strengths: many content teachers at Hancock valued reading and writing, and they made a strong effort to provide reteaching and extension to students who needed differentiation.

Student Interaction and Understanding

There is great value in having the opportunity to speak with students during classroom visits. Although student interaction data are subjective, they can provide a deeper context for the data collected from the classroom visits.

During the Hancock LVCCs, visitors were able to speak with students in about 38 percent of the classrooms. Of those students, nearly all of them could explain the learning goals or targets (see Figure 7.6). On the other hand, only about half of the students said that they felt secure in reading the assigned texts and had opportunities to discuss texts and ideas with their peers. Students reported that most of their peer conversations occurred during whole-group sharing, although they occasionally met in small groups to work on projects.

Figure 7.6 | *Hancock's Student Interaction and Understanding Data*

Student Interaction and Understanding	
82%	Students know what they are supposed to learn and demonstrate.
48%	Students have an opportunity to talk with peers about their reading and learning.
52%	Students are able to read and understand the texts on their own.
62%	N/A (Student not available for questions; observers spoke with students in 38% of classrooms).

What Effective Literacy Instruction Looks Like in the Content Classroom

The following two anecdotes put together the six components of the LVCC instrument to form the whole picture of what effective literacy instruction and learning look like in a real content-area classroom.

A Visit to a Middle School Science Classroom

Ms. Raphael teaches middle school science in a school of about 800 students. Her classroom has clearly designated areas for community learning in whole group, a small table for small-group meetings, and enough space for students to read in comfortable places. The desks are grouped into pods of four to six, which facilitates science labs and other group work.

Ms. Raphael's classroom library, where a shelving unit houses bins of labeled, differentiated science texts, speaks to her strong interest in science. Students also have access to electronic texts and science apps on their tablets. A large bulletin board houses science vocabulary words. Students add to the word wall regularly and use the words in their speaking and writing. Another wall shares examples of lab work, projects, and photographs of students engaged in science experiments. Students keep science notebooks along with self-selected science texts in individual book bins.

The learning targets for today's lesson incorporate a science standard with a reading and a writing standard: *I can identify all the parts of a plant cell by reading about them, making and labeling an edible cell, and drawing the model in my notebook.* Students will be following directions to complete a hands-on activity and recording their work and observations in their writing notebooks.

Continued

Ms. Raphael leads a short explanatory lesson and uses a video to introduce the key vocabulary. She involves students in this process by using several responsive techniques, including having them use individual whiteboards to respond to group questions and engage in peer discussion to reach consensus on those responses.

Next, students browse informational texts that they had selected earlier based on their instructional level or interest. After students have been given a few minutes to skim a book of their choice about cells, Ms. Raphael asks them to write down a question or statement about something that they are interested in exploring more deeply or that sparks their curiosity.

Ms. Raphael then asks students to select and read one of three different readings that she provided to explain the parts of the cells. She created three text-dependent questions to focus students' purpose for reading. When they finish reading, she informs them that they will have materials on their tables to construct an edible cell in small groups. After they construct their cells, they will need to identify the parts by stating them accurately to one leader within the group. Finally, they will use their knowledge from the reading and hands-on activity to draw and label a cell in their notebooks. One designated student in each group writes key vocabulary terms on notecards and adds them to the word wall.

During the hands-on activity, students follow a specific lab protocol that is posted in the classroom near the lab area. Their familiarity in moving through the process clearly shows that they have used it often and can work well both in groups and on their own.

Ms. Raphael carries her tablet with her as she observes each group, using questions to prompt and guide their process as she makes notes of individual and group behaviors and responses. She uses these data, along with the student work in their science notebooks, to group students for future activities as well as to review her lesson planning and consider opportunities to differentiate.

As students finish, they read self-selected science texts that support the concepts and goals of the day. Ms. Raphael meets with several students one-on-one and asks them to share their lab notes or talk about the texts they are reading. She provides feedback to these individual students and makes additional notes in her tablet.

A Visit to a High School Social Studies Classroom

Mr. Clifton teaches 9th and 10th grade social studies. His classroom is set up differently from a traditional high school classroom: there is a resource area with several bookshelves that hold texts, social studies magazines, journals, and other resources; a table with several computer stations to access research; and a set of tablets for portable use. The walls of the room indicate that students make decisions about the vocabulary, strategy charts, and student work that are displayed. Wall charts visually explain expectations for small-group and independent work behaviors. Movable desks on wheels, which can be positioned separately for independent work or into pods for small-group work, serve as work stations for students.

Mr. Clifton's 9th grade class is learning about U.S. history. Today is Wednesday, so this is the third lesson in the unit with a set of weekly goals. The learning targets for the lesson focus on identifying and understanding major events and turning points in U.S. history and the impact that these critical events had on the American Revolution. The performance criterion is to develop an annotated timeline of 8–10 events, supported with citations from several texts and electronic primary and secondary sources. Students will be using the results of this task and other assignments to analyze aspects of the American Revolution later in the unit, so Mr. Clifton notes this fact next to the posted learning targets. He also has printed the standards that the lesson addresses next to the posted learning targets.

Continued

Mr. Clifton then delivers a mini-lesson on how to electronically access a primary-source document related to a specific historic event while students record the steps. He models how he would skim the text to find the sections related to his focus. Reading the identified sections, he highlights important words and concepts. When he reaches the end, he asks students to select one highlighted area and write why they believe it was worthy of note. Then he asks students to share their thoughts with a peer while he moves through the room listening and viewing their notes.

Returning to the interactive whiteboard, he unpacks a highlighted segment of the text, modeling a think-aloud of how it provides information and context that he can use when creating his timeline. Then he models how he uses textual evidence to support his learning and cites the work that he plans to use. He repeats this process using another section of the text, but this time asks students to unpack a highlighted area and think aloud with a peer, using the process he has modeled earlier in this lesson. Next, he reviews the learning target and connects the performance criterion to the lesson he just modeled. After checking in to make sure all class members know what they are supposed to do next, students are released to work.

Students work either on their own or in groups of two or three. Each group meets to determine how it will construct its timeline and who is responsible for gathering which element before rejoining the group. Mr. Clifton has a schedule posted of meetings with groups and individuals, and he keeps a record of individual contributions to the group as well as the group's ability to function. Students are also expected to assess the group's process as well as their contributions as group members. They are aware of these expectations and work well. Between meetings with students, Mr. Clifton checks in briefly with groups and individuals to make sure they are engaged and moving forward with their work.

Mr. Clifton's students are palpably excited about their class. They feel it is their classroom and they have decision-making power within it. They shared that Mr. Clifton is aware of their reading needs and offers alternative options for students who need support. Groups are reassigned regularly and are not based solely on ability; student interest and need for developing work behaviors are also a part of the grouping process. Students related that in addition to learning about history, they are learning how to cooperate in groups and work to meet goals and deadlines.

The Right Tools for the Job

Both the Literacy Classroom Visit instrument and the Literacy Visit in the Content Classroom instrument are tools for analyzing the culture of overall instruction and learning in a school or district. Both honor the need to communicate clear instructional goals to students, teach the content across the gradual release of responsibility, and differentiate to address individual student needs. The LCV form can be used specifically in language arts classrooms, while the LVCC instrument is universal. These tools lay the foundation for collecting rich data about resource and professional learning needs in a school while giving leaders the flexibility to unpack, revise, adapt, or enhance the focus of any instrument.

Reflection to Action

- How can you establish an LCV process with the educators in your school or district?
- What do you need to do to prepare your teachers and your leadership team for the process?
- How will you use the LCV data with student achievement data to plan for professional learning in your school?
- How will you work with your district to align your school's professional learning plans with district professional development goals?

PART III:
Creating a Unified System

SCENARIO: BEL AIR ELEMENTARY SCHOOL

Our journey began when Mounds View School District's 10 elementary school administrators attended 4 days of literacy leadership training focused on the Literacy Classroom Visit Model. By concentrating on balanced literacy in each school's PLCs throughout our school district, we have begun to discuss the different components on the LCV instrument. We are using the data from our visits to consider strengths around balanced literacy and to establish literacy plans to address identified needs.

As the principal at Bel Air, I have worked closely with our school's leadership team and literacy coach in reviewing the data from our LCV. Together, we learned from our data that independent reading for students could be enhanced. We also determined that to expect students to read with stamina, classrooms would need well-stocked libraries. To address these identified needs, we used some of our school's federal funds to purchase about 100 nonfiction titles for each teacher's classroom library this year, and we have begun to address professional needs by studying and working on learning targets.

This new journey as a district and as an elementary principal group has led to purposeful conversations that keep the learning leadership role in the forefront of our daily work. In addition, the transformations I have seen in classrooms with the alignment of learning targets, demonstration of learning, and daily routines around independent reading are amazing! Students are deeply engaged in reading, and they are writing about what they are reading.

When I asked a 4th grade student how his reading class is different this year from last year, his comment was, "We have a classroom library this year; and we read a lot more!"

I don't believe I would have been as ready to support the literacy development work in my school without having attended the literacy leadership training and using the LCV resources. This strong foundation helps me recognize best practice in literacy instruction when I visit classrooms and gives me confidence to lead my staff in providing best practice literacy instruction for our students.

Dawn Wiegand, Principal
Bel Air Elementary School
New Brighton, Minnesota

Using the Literacy Classroom Visit Model Across a School District

8

Improvement requires new and different two-way relationships between each school and the district, and new relationships across schools as the district develops a new professional learning culture in the entire district.

—Michael Fullan, *Whole School Reform: Problems and Promises*

Using the Literacy Classroom Visit Model in a single school fosters a literacy culture within that building and contributes to the excellent instruction that already exists. However, using the model in only one school of many within a school district reduces its potential to effect lasting systemwide change. The most effective way to implement the LCV Model is through a districtwide initiative, where the data can contribute to district strategic plans and provide direction for action and improvement.

The District Role in School Improvement

Many school districts across the United States contain some excellent schools, yet it is difficult to find a single large district where these schools are the norm rather than the exception (Mehta, Hess, & Schwartz, 2011). In the past, education leaders advised that the school, as opposed to the district, should be the central focus for reform (Marzano, 2003; Reynolds & Teddlie, 2000). As a result, many districts have focused on directing school-based efforts to increase student achievement rather than setting broader, districtwide goals.

This propensity to focus on the parts rather than the whole has created some persistent issues in education, including the widespread misperception that district staff members have little responsibility for school-level improvement efforts. A review of the research (Leithwood & Seashore-Louis, 2011) found that the chance of success of any school's or district's effort to improve student learning is remote unless *all* leaders agree with its purposes and appreciate what is required to make it work. District-level leadership is critical to improving student learning and school improvement.

Within the context of this book, one of the major roles of central office leaders is to build capacity within the school district by developing school administrators' ability to promote high-quality literacy instruction. In this capacity, the central office should support building leaders in using data to make decisions, developing a foundational understanding of the research-based practices that teachers must implement to support student growth, understanding the LCV Model for literacy improvement, and designing evaluation methods to assess the degree to which professional learning has improved student achievement. Through these capacity-building efforts, district leaders take on a supportive and collaborative role.

If the LCV Model is part of a multischool initiative, district leaders can help ensure that all school leaders conduct useful and powerful Literacy Classroom Visits. They can accomplish this task by providing professional learning for principals and teacher leaders from each school, conducting LCVs in small groups and analyzing the data together, offering coaching, and providing additional access to outside experts when needed.

The LCV Role in Supporting District Plans

Just as the support of district leaders can help ensure effective implementation of the LCV Model, the converse is also true: the LCV process can help coordinate and focus districtwide improvement efforts, providing a research-based model for taking action.

Schools and districts are required to have improvement plans that specify instructional and curricular ideas to enhance teachers' ongoing practice and assist students in performing at higher levels. Successful schools and districts also design and implement professional learning plans to ensure that teachers have the training and support necessary to provide instruction that is current, research based, and effective. An effective district literacy plan coordinates and supports school-based literacy goals and unifies schools' efforts into a cohesive structure (Irvin, Meltzer, Dean, & Mickler, 2010). A strong plan also indicates the types of student performance data being collected and how the data will be used.

On the other hand, elaborate school improvement plans that do not focus exclusively and directly on curriculum implementation and instructional improvement are not helpful to improving student achievement (Schmoker, 2006). Many districts do not have clear classroom data that focus on literacy culture and the actual instructional practices being implemented in each school, but understanding these elements is crucial for success. This is where the Literacy Classroom Visit Model can make a difference. Using the LCV data from each school in a district can provide a richer, more comprehensive view of the status of teaching and learning in the district as well as in each school. These data can be used to design improvement plans and help outline the best strategies for reaching district and school goals.

In an effective district plan, each comprehensive goal outlines the specific steps and strategies needed for success. Figure 8.1 provides an example of one goal that focuses on building the leadership capacity of principals and teacher leaders by providing professional learning about the LCV Model and offering support for its use during the year. Other goals in the improvement plan may focus on additional areas of need as identified by various data sources. For example, one need may be to develop foundational knowledge in balanced literacy instruction and the gradual release of responsibility. As educators implement the strategies, data are collected by leaders or coaches using different measures, including the LCV and enhanced LCV instruments or check-ins, to monitor progress and adjust implementation strategies. We advocate that districts implement the LCV Model in all schools and provide professional learning for district, school, and teacher leaders on how to implement and use it effectively.

The Role of District Leaders in Implementing the LCV Model

We've established that districts are the logical avenue to provide the support that school leaders need to improve literacy teaching and learning. Ensuring that schools get what they need without causing undue frustration requires a balanced partnership and clarity between districts and schools. On the one hand, entrusting the job solely to

Figure 8.1 | *Improvement Plan Goal Example*

Goal	Task or Activity	Time Line	Person(s) Responsible	Resources	Evidence of Success
Literacy leadership teams from each school will learn to use the LCV Model effectively to collect data and analyze patterns that emerge.	Identify teacher leaders for each school who understand and can articulate the effective components of literacy teaching and student learning.	Spring of preceding year	Principals	Participation in literacy-focused professional learning, observation data indicating effectiveness	Formation of teams
	Provide professional development to teacher leaders on the use of the LCV Model.	Summer and ongoing during the school year	District leaders or outside consultants	Time to meet in summer and six times during the school year, substitute coverage	Meeting agendas, LCV data, notes from LCVs, teacher surveys, evaluations
	Create opportunities for classroom teachers to use the LCV instruments.	At minimum: fall, winter, spring	District leaders, principals, teacher leaders	Time to conduct a minimum of three LCVs in a school year, substitute coverage	LCV data, notes from LCVs
	Create opportunities to discuss and analyze data patterns and plan next steps.	Following each round of LCVs	District leaders, principals, teacher leaders	Time to discuss and plan professional learning after each LCV in a school year, substitute coverage	LCV data, notes from LCVs, data analysis instrument

principals often results in a fragmented process. On the other hand, district administrators who impose mandates and deliver uniform professional learning to all schools within their purview will likely see their improvement efforts fail. District administrators who create a learning environment based on trust and clearly established norms for collaboration create a culture in which the LCV Model can bear fruit.

In effective districts, central office administrators are continually working to increase their support of professional learning throughout the district and to effectively respond to schools' particular needs. They explicitly model the learning and risk taking that are essential to effective change as they reform their own practice.

District leadership, according to the Learning Forward (2011) Standards for Professional Learning, should provide professional learning experiences that enable principals to function as instructional leaders.

Learning Forward has placed this expectation on district leadership because a unified professional development plan that is focused, job-embedded, and sustained has the potential to make the greatest impact.

As far as the LCV Model goes, district leaders and principals have distinct, mutually reinforcing roles. The central office assumes responsibility for defining goals and standards for teaching and learning, allocating resources to schools, and providing the supports that principals and teachers need to successfully meet district-established literacy standards. Principals and teachers are responsible for implementing teaching and learning goals, using school-based professional development resources, and developing strategies for evaluating their progress. To effectively implement Literacy Classroom Visits, district and school leaders must

- Ensure successful training and ongoing support for conducting LCVs.
- Provide consistent structures for analyzing LCV data to determine professional learning needs and the impact such learning is having on instruction and student learning.
- Model the delivery of nonevaluative, effective feedback about the LCV to teachers to inspire growth and change.
- Offer strategies for providing the professional learning identified by LCV data as needed to improve literacy instruction.
- Guide the use of LCV data to monitor the implementation of the knowledge and practices gained through professional learning experiences.

District leaders can also assist with schools' collection, analysis, and use of LCV data for decision making. Specifically, districts can help schools improve the validity, reliability, and relevance of the LCV data collected and provide technical assistance or training opportunities in using the data to inform management, instruction, and literacy improvement. Data are not helpful if users don't know how to access them, don't trust them, or don't have time to analyze them.

Finally, district leaders can give principals opportunities to meet to share and learn about strategies and approaches that support quality teaching. This collegial work is as important for administrators as it is for teachers. By providing this time, district leaders help principals learn from one another and work toward realistic and practical leadership strategy application of the LCV Model.

Professional Learning for Principals: Collaboration and Coaching

The best way to grow a district's capacity to improve teaching and learning is to ensure that every school becomes a model of effective professional learning through collaboration and collegiality. To increase their effectiveness in raising student achievement, principals need opportunities to participate in learning opportunities with their peers (Mizell, 2009).

One way to build leaders' capacity to work effectively together is by developing a cadre of principals and other leaders who work with learning teams within their schools. For principals to understand, value, and lead these learning teams, they need to experience working within facilitated study teams themselves.

It works best to use small-group learning structures; in small groups, principals feel safe asking questions and seeking help from one another. Their learning teams should focus on promoting instructional leadership; understanding, facilitating, and determining the effectiveness of professional learning communities; and identifying, supporting, and providing feedback on quality teaching. **Video 8.1** provides an example of what this looks like, showing principals attending a four-day Literacy Academy where they learn about the LCV Model and other related literacy information to enhance their instructional leadership skills.

Lakeville's literacy visits over the past year have helped our administrative team become more intentional and focused on the specific components of an effective balanced literacy model. With the support of our literacy consultants, we have created a consistent protocol of look-fors in each component. A common language around literacy is beginning to develop as a result of doing these visits together as a leadership team throughout the district. Our literacy visits are different from our normal walkthroughs, as we are collecting data looking for trends in our overall system. The trends we find will help target future district and site professional development. I appreciate that we—literacy consultants, district leaders, and staff—are on this journey together as we continue to become even more effective literacy educators.

Pete Otterson, Principal

Professional learning for principals must provide the opportunity to examine important areas specific to the culture and context they lead. To make learning teams effective, district administrators can provide principals with ongoing experiences to learn about aligning literacy instruction to best practices and using data in group decision making.

Conducting LCVs with district literacy leaders is, in itself, useful professional learning for principals. Their discussions about the attributes identified on the LCV instrument help them identify what is being taught, and the process of identifying and communicating areas of strength and need deepens their content knowledge and enhances their ability to hold meaningful and focused conversations with teachers about their instruction and student learning.

District leaders should also schedule a skilled group facilitator to coach principals during learning team meetings. On-site coaching is a powerful strategy that can deepen school leaders' commitment and will to change and strengthen their instructional leadership skills. Some coaching efforts focus only on school and district leaders, whereas others work with a broader constituency within the school system. For example, when the coach conducts an LCV within a school, he or she may offer assistance and feedback to the teacher leaders who are conducting the visits with the principal. This option develops the leadership skills of both teacher leaders and principals.

Coaching often helps school leaders focus on whole-school improvement and content coaching to facilitate the improvement of literacy instruction. The goal of this special coaching is to implement the LCV Model and guide schools while helping to build principals' and teacher leaders' capacity to do this work on their own.

Building a community of leaders is vital to improving instructional leadership. As leaders work together to learn and discuss developing practices, they create relationships that have a positive effect on those whom they lead (Spillane, 2006). As teachers see their leaders working and growing together, they respond to the model of collaboration.

A Districtwide Culture of Literacy

Districts play numerous important roles in promoting and sustaining the successful use of the LCV Model. When district leaders assume the responsibility of building capacity through their school leaders, they develop a collaborative culture that supports application of the LCV Model and builds a flourishing literacy environment. In **Video 8.2**, principals talk about the value of using the LCV Model throughout their school district.

Reflection to Action

- How can the Literacy Classroom Visit Model support and extend your district's strategic plan, literacy improvement plan, or professional learning plan?
- How might you collaborate with other school and district leaders to use the LCV Model?

Conclusion

The Literacy Classroom Visit process promotes reflective practice and meaningful conversations among educators.

—Julie Davis, Executive Director, Ohio Association
of Elementary Administrators

One of the most important purposes of schooling is to develop wise readers and critical thinkers. To achieve this purpose, school leaders must become literacy leaders and plan strategically for improvement. This complex goal, in turn, requires a system that enables leaders to collect and analyze timely and useful information about the current status of literacy instruction and learning in their schools and districts and to evaluate how well students are engaging in the process of literacy learning. These tasks are what we designed the Literacy Classroom Visit Model for.

With their focus on improving the classroom environment and literacy instruction to support and extend student achievement, Literacy Classroom Visits are seated in research-based practices that are necessary to help students become critical thinkers, effective readers, and meaning makers.

To sum up, the Literacy Classroom Visit Model

- Provides a tool kit for introducing the process to the school community, creating understanding and buy-in among the school community, and collecting initial data and evidence around the six key areas of effective literacy instruction.
- Yields clear data on a school's or district's literacy culture and instructional practices that can be used to design improvement plans, identify the best strategies for reaching district and school

goals, and document evidence of a developing literacy culture and established instructional practices.

- Deepens leaders' content knowledge, enhancing their ability to hold meaningful and focused conversations with teachers about instruction and student development.

- Helps central office leaders build capacity within the school district by developing school administrators' skills in promoting quality literacy instruction.

Finding the "sweet spot" among what research says about effective instruction, what teachers know and are doing in classrooms, and how these important elements intersect with student development can be challenging. However, finding this critical intersection is a catalyst for lasting change. The Literacy Classroom Visit Model provides a solid vehicle to uncover and deal productively with this information.

APPENDIX A:
Information About Literacy Classroom Visits

Literacy Classroom Visits in a Nutshell

The Literacy Classroom Visit Model was developed by Bonnie D. Houck, EdD, and Sandi Novak to assist educators in establishing a process to support continuous improvement in literacy instruction and learning. The model promotes inquiry and reflective practice focused on student growth and achievement in a school or district. Its central tool is the Literacy Classroom Visit instrument, which guides educators in noting specific literacy look-fors.

The purpose of Literacy Classroom Visits is to document observed evidence of a developing classroom culture of literacy as well as research-supported literacy instructional practices. Instruments designed for this purpose enable LCV teams to collect data during several classroom visits in a building before reviewing and analyzing the data and providing feedback for inquiry and decision making.

Data collected through Literacy Classroom Visits can be helpful in discussing the areas of strength and need in a school's continuous efforts to foster a culture of literacy. The school community receives feedback at the school and grade levels. Data are used not to evaluate or to focus on the practices of individual teachers but to identify the patterns that indicate the school's strengths and needs in its continuous journey to meet the literacy learning needs of all students.

Collecting LCV data over time can

- Establish a body of evidence about a school's or district's overall literacy culture and instruction.
- Identify instructional patterns within teacher teams, grade levels, and content areas.
- Pinpoint resource needs and reduce unnecessary budget expenditures.
- Guide planning for professional learning and PLC team content.
- Establish common beliefs, practices, and language within the community.
- Inform a school community about the implementation of professional learning goals.
- Ensure that students are learning and mastering grade-level standards and expectations.

The focus of the observable classroom artifacts and instructional behaviors is literacy—specifically, reading instruction. Classroom visits are brief, lasting approximately three to five minutes, although they may be longer when a school is first implementing the model. A research-based recording instrument is used to keep consistent records and anecdotal notes.

Every effort is taken to document all that was observed. That said, if an area is not noted as observed during the visit, it does not mean that the area is not present at other times during the literacy block; it just means that it was not observed at that time. It should be noted that these data come from one snapshot in time. A continuous process of classroom visits will build an album of these snapshots that tell the story of a school's literacy learning journey.

Literacy Classroom Visit Protocol

Group Norms

- Our purpose is to learn and grow professionally, not to evaluate others.
- We will uphold norms of confidentiality about the visits.
- We will provide explicit, nonjudgmental evidence when collecting, reviewing, and sharing data.

Classroom Visits

- Our goal is to avoid distractions to the class.
- We will enter the classroom quietly and find an unobtrusive spot to observe from.
- We will refrain from conversation with the classroom teacher or other team members.
- We will ensure that each class visit is for a consistent duration of three to five minutes.

Gathering Data and Supporting Evidence

- Our goal is to record factual data on what we see, using specific evidence ("I heard . . . I saw . . .") and refraining from subjective statements ("I liked . . .").
- We will reflect on the use of space, anchor charts, and student work on display.
- When appropriate, we will ask students one to two questions ("What is the learning target? Why are you learning it? How do you know if your work is good? What do you do if you need help?").
- We will wait to ask clarifying questions in the hall after the first classroom visit if the components on the instrument are unclear.

Individual Reflection

- We will individually and silently review all notes and evidence collected during the classroom visits.
- We will review and revise notes to ensure that they are nonjudgmental and specific.
- We will individually highlight the data and supporting evidence directly linked to the area of focus.

Debriefing the Classroom Visits

- Everyone will be given the opportunity to share highlights and supporting evidence linked to the area of focus.
- We will reach consensus on strengths and areas in need of support.
- We will compose summary statements to share with staff.

Discussing the Components of Literacy Classroom Visits

In this section, we walk you through the look-fors for each of the six key areas of effective literacy instruction found in the LCV instrument. We hope this helps you plan and launch enriching, insightful discussions about your school's culture and practice to support continuous improvement.

Classroom Environment and Culture

A classroom's physical arrangement and organization can powerfully support or unintentionally impede effective literacy instruction (Morrow, Reutzel, & Casey, 2006; Reutzel, Jones, & Newman, 2010; Reutzel & Morrow, 2007; Wolfersberger, Reutzel, Sudweeks, & Fawson, 2004). A literacy-supportive classroom environment has many elements, but we have identified seven crucial areas. We briefly describe each area below and include reflective questions to support an internal conversation about the strengths and possible needs of your classroom environment and use of physical space.

Classroom structure and practices support a developing culture of literacy. A balanced literacy classroom supports the gradual release model of instruction. The physical space of the classroom allows for efficient transitions from whole-group to small-group to independent learning settings. The majority of the classroom floor space is clearly designated for student learning.

> **Reflective Questions:**
>
> Walk into your classroom with new eyes. Does the classroom inform a visitor that it highly values reading and writing? Does the physical space support literacy development? Is there a balance in how instruction is delivered? What percentage of the classroom space is used by the teacher? Set aside for the students? What are students doing? Are expectations and goals posted?

Students are actively and purposefully engaged in literacy-focused learning activities. Students are reading self-selected texts, texts to prepare for guided reading, and texts that extend the learning from class. Students are writing in response to reading and learning or writing creatively or through a process. Students are discussing literature and one another's writing. Students are actively working in literacy development centers or stations. Students are engaged in technology experiences that support and extend literacy development.

Reflective Questions:

Do the activities support literacy development? Are the activities supported by explicit instruction and modeling and guided practice? Does the learning that results from this work expand students' literacy knowledge and skills? Is this work a worthwhile use of students' time?

Classroom library is organized to support self-selection and class size/level (300+ texts). The classroom library is an important resource for a balanced literacy classroom. A functional classroom library has, at minimum, 10–12 books per student. The texts are high quality and represent a balance of fiction and informational texts in a variety of genres and informational text structures. E-books and audiobooks can also be a wonderful part of the classroom library. The books are arranged in an organized fashion that supports student self-selection. The library includes leveled texts, but the organization should offer a variety of ways to view and choose texts from content-area bins featuring developmentally appropriate labels, favorite author and series texts, chapter books in alphabetical order, and informational texts organized by topic or Dewey Decimal numerals. The classroom library area is appealing and has a process for choosing texts and for developing a book bag or bin for independent reading time. The library includes books that are appropriate for students reading at, above, or below grade level.

Reflective Questions:

Is the classroom library area inviting? Approximately how many books are in the library? How are they arranged? What processes are established for self-selecting texts (such as IPICK or BOOKMATCH), assembling individual book bins, and refreshing book bins as students finish reading texts?

Classroom library has a balance of fiction/informational texts at varied levels. The Common Core standards challenge us to teach both literature and informational text and text features and structures at increasing levels of difficulty. Classroom libraries must support these goals so that students can practice what we teach them when they read on their own. In every classroom, students' reading ranges can differ greatly. A classroom library must have enough texts for each student to keep a book bin.

Reflective Questions:

Does the classroom library have a balance of fiction and informational texts? Does the collection span the reading range of the students in that classroom? Are texts organized in a way that enables students to choose and exchange texts efficiently?

Rituals, routines, and procedures are in place. The rituals, routines, and responsibilities of a balanced literacy classroom provide the structure for students to become self-motivated, self-directed learners. The walls of the classroom speak to these important processes through anchor charts or I-Charts that identify the engagement and behaviors necessary during each aspect of the gradual release. Students and teachers agree on what it looks like, sounds like, and feels like when they are doing their job during whole-group, small-group, paired, and independent aspects of instruction and learning. Transitions of movement from whole-group to small-group to independent learning modes are timely and purposeful. During the first month of school, development of rituals and routines is essential, as is the building of stamina to read independently for up to 30 minutes every day.

Reflective Questions:

Are there student-generated informational charts indicating what it "looks like" when students are doing what is expected? Are transitions smooth and timely? Do students know their role and the teacher's role? Are they actively and purposefully engaged?

Displays of student work show development and celebrate literacy learning. The walls of the classroom tell a story. The examples of student work portray students' development and progress, celebrate their hard work, and provide a sense of ownership and community.

Reflective Questions:

Is student work a part of the classroom environment? Does it inform visitors about the classroom's instruction and students' literacy development? Is it current?

Interactive word walls are used to support writing and vocabulary development. A word wall is an ongoing, organized display of key words that provides visual reference for students throughout a term or unit of study. Teachers and students use these words continually during a variety of activities. Word walls must be consistent across grade levels. Word walls serve multiple purposes. Effective word walls

- Support the teaching of key words and subject-specific terminology.
- Promote independence in reading and writing by building vocabulary.
- Foster student reading and writing development and provide a resource for transitioning from invented to conventional spelling.
- Provide visual clues and reference for English language learners.
- Help students remember connections between words and concepts.

Reflective Questions:

Do the primary classrooms have sight word/write word "word walls"? Do intermediate classrooms use word walls to support and extend vocabulary development? Is there a shared philosophy at and across grade levels? Are there consistent expectations for how students will use the words? Do the words support the student literacy goals and expectations for reading and writing?

Learning Target/Instructional Goal

A learning target is a statement of intended learning based on the standards. A learning target specifies and unpacks the objective and spells out what students will be able to do during and after the lesson or lesson series. Learning targets are written in student-friendly language, are specific to the lesson for the day or span of days, and are directly connected to assessment. A standard answers the question "Where am I going in my learning?" Learning targets show students the path to get there. Learning targets are student-centered and guide student learning. A lesson with a clear learning target clearly and articulately states the purpose of the lesson in a way that will empower students to *know, learn, do,* and *show.*

Effective learning targets are posted and visible in the learning area, identify the performance criteria, and are taught and supported through the gradual release of responsibility. The teacher explicitly teaches and models the learning target in whole group, coaches students in applying it while reading and writing during small-group guided practice, and assesses students' development in meeting performance criteria on their own. The teacher can assess the performance criteria through observation, conferring, or evaluation using a rubric, checklist, or other tool. In some cases, the demonstration of learning can be a piece of writing, a quiz or a test, a project, or another product.

Reflective Questions:

Is the learning target posted and visible? Is it clearly articulated in student-friendly language? Is it aligned to standards? Does it explain the demonstration of learning (performance criteria)?

Observed Method of Instructional Delivery

The Literacy Classroom Visit takes about three to five minutes in each classroom. During that time, the observers note the method of instructional delivery that was used by the teacher. If the teacher is working with the entire class, "whole-group lesson" will be noted; if the teacher is leading small groups, "small-group lesson" will be noted; and if the teacher is conferring with students, "independent reading and application" will be noted.

Whole-Group Explicit Instruction

Whole-group reading instruction is the teacher's opportunity to

- Orally and visually share the learning target (the objective of the lesson, which is often the reading strategy), the steps to successfully reach the learning target, and the demonstration of learning, or what students will do to show the teacher they know and understand the learning target (assessment).
- Explicitly teach and model the learning target.

The teacher does this by selecting, reading, and rereading books at grade level or above to expose students to a wide variety of quality texts, language, and rich vocabulary. The teacher uses strategic times to stop, model, and think aloud to explicitly show how a wise reader applies and uses the learning target, other reading strategies, and higher-order thinking skills.

During whole-group reading instruction, students

- Participate and actively respond to instruction and learning.
- Focus attention on fiction, nonfiction, skills, strategy, and other forms of instruction.
- Ask questions and answer the teacher's questions.
- Clarify learning with a partner.
- Respond to and participate in the development of written response, sticky notes, graphic organizers, or other tools that foster engagement in the lesson.

The following sections discuss three essential elements of whole-group instruction and include reflective questions to guide discussion about whole-group instruction in your school.

Teacher is leading a focused mini-lesson or lesson using time effectively for age range. A clear learning target guides the lesson, providing focus to ensure the best use of instructional time. Jensen (2005) asserts that students can maintain attention in whole-group settings for the number of minutes equaling their age plus two. So, an average 3rd grader can benefit from whole-group lessons that deliver content for about 10–12 minutes before he or she needs to interact with a peer or independently reflect on and respond to learning. Whole-group sessions should balance the explicit instruction and modeling of new learning, with guided questions and responses and opportunities to interact with peers or respond in writing.

> ### Reflective Questions:
>
> Is the teacher using the time effectively? Has the teacher provided time for students to respond to both teacher and peers? Are the techniques used for student engagement and interaction effective?

Teacher is explicitly teaching/modeling effective skill/strategy (learning target). Explicit instruction is a structured, systematic, effective, and direct approach to teaching that includes both instructional design and delivery procedures. Explicit instruction starts with a learning target or goal for the lesson that is aligned to standards. The teacher studies the standard across several grade levels in order to understand the supporting knowledge students need and the next steps required to apply the standard. The teacher unwraps the learning in order to develop supports, scaffolds, and extensions to guide students through the learning process.

> ### Reflective Questions:
>
> Is the teacher explicitly teaching and modeling or just explaining, questioning, and assigning? Is the learning target or skill/strategy clearly explained, unpacked, and modeled so that students know what it is and what they need to do?

Students are actively listening, purposefully engaged, and interacting with teacher and peers. During whole group, students can sit and listen for a defined period of time before disengaging. Student engagement can range from complete disengagement, to passive engagement, to active purposeful engagement. It is critical that the teacher employ responsive activities that can connect with students and assess engagement and understanding during whole group, such as using "fist to five" to check understanding; using whiteboards to quickly display learning; and using pair-share, prompting elbow-to-elbow conversations, or moving around to ascertain the level of understanding among the group. Active engagement and response goes beyond responding to teacher questions and provides opportunities for students to share their knowledge with their peers.

> **Reflective Questions:**
>
> Do the students know what they are supposed to do during whole group? Is the lesson content developmentally appropriate? Is the teacher integrating student interaction beyond individual responses to teacher questions? Are student conversations relevant to the content and focus of the lesson?

Small-Group Guided Practice

Small-group reading instruction provides the teacher with the opportunity to coach and guide students while they practice applying the learning targets and reading skills and strategies explicitly taught and modeled in whole-group reading instruction using texts at their instructional level. Teachers collect and study formative and summative data regularly to flexibly group students. There are several effective ways to do small-group reading instruction during Tier 1 (core instruction) during the 90- to 120-minute literacy block in a balanced literacy classroom, including

- Guided reading.
- Flexible strategy groups.
- Tier 1/core instruction intervention and reteaching groups.
- Student-led discussion groups (including reciprocal teaching groups and literature circles).

A teacher can use one or more of these grouping strategies to meet students' needs.

The teacher's role during this part of the gradual release of responsibility is to

- Flexibly group students according to specific learning needs related to the lesson.
- Scaffold instructional tasks so that students are challenged but feel competent and capable of addressing the task with the support of the teacher and other members of the small group.

- Coach and support small groups of students reading texts at their instructional level.
- Guide students and listen to them read as they apply skills and strategies modeled in whole group.
- Specifically discuss key words, concepts, and strategies that support developmental literacy learning.
- Engage students in interactive conversations, encouraging participation with peers.

NOTE: Round Robin reading is *not* supported by research! Nor is "popcorn" reading or the use of Popsicle sticks to take turns reading aloud. Grouping students by level or ability during core instruction for prolonged periods of time is *not* supported by research either. Finally, for students to be successful in student-led discussion groups, the teacher must explicitly teach and model each component of the small-group discussion before releasing students to work independently.

The following sections discuss four essential elements of small-group guided practice and include reflective questions to guide discussion about it in your school.

Teacher is guiding students' reading, strategy application, and collaborative discussions. The teacher provides a quick review and reading of the learning target, asking students if they understand what they are to work on and demonstrate. The teacher selects instructional-level texts so that students can practice the skill/strategy within the context of reading and discussing texts.

Reflective Questions:

Is the teacher doing a quick review of whole group or repeating a whole-group lesson in small group? Does the teacher ask students to reread or review the learning target and demonstration of learning? Is the lesson focus part of the gradual release of the learning target? Who is talking the most: the teacher or the students?

Teacher is listening to students read while assessing strengths/needs and collecting anecdotal notes. The teacher regularly asks students to read silently or whisper read while he or she listens to individual students read and apply the learning target. The teacher has a method of collecting data on the students' reading development and application of skills and strategies that informs instruction and grouping practices.

Reflective Questions:

Is the teacher sitting close to the students while reading, recording data, or providing individual feedback? What are other students doing as the teacher listens to one student read? Are they reading silently?

Students are reading and discussing texts at their instructional level. Guided reading provides the opportunity to practice the learning target and develop reading skills and strategies with the support of the teacher. Students can use texts that are more challenging with extra guidance.

Reflective Questions:

Does the teacher provide text-dependent questions to set the purpose and guide the reading? Do the students use the question prompts to collaboratively discuss the text?

Students are practicing the skill or strategy explicitly taught and modeled in whole group. The teacher selects instructional-level texts so that students can practice the skill/strategy within the context of reading and discussing texts. Students use sticky notes, graphic organizers, and other tools to practice learning targets and demonstrate learning.

Reflective Questions:

Are the students reading/using instructional-level texts? Are they appropriate resources for practicing the skill/strategy? Did the teacher provide supports or tools such as graphic organizers or sticky notes to assist students in strategy application? Is the application aligned to the learning target?

Independent Reading and Application

Independent reading is a nonnegotiable 30 minutes of daily reading of self-selected books. Students have developed strategies to self-select texts at their independent to instructional levels that meet their interests and purposes for reading, providing opportunities to stretch and hone their reading skills and strategies. This daily practice encourages students to become self-motivated, self-directed, engaged readers who are critical thinkers, problem solvers, and meaning makers who *love* and choose to read!

How do students become wise readers? They *read*—a lot, every day. They read books that they choose and want to read, as well as texts provided by teachers and parents. How do teachers become wise reading teachers? We know our partners in the process. Byrnes (2000) asserted that teachers will not enhance student achievement simply by allocating more time to silent reading; rather, they need to provide instructional scaffolds (Baker, 2002). Just scheduling the time to read self-selected books every day is *not* enough. Teachers must set up

- A nonnegotiable time for students to read every day.
- A process for choosing "just right" books.
- A system for building and maintaining book bins or bags.
- A way for students to keep track of the genres and types of informational texts they have been reading.
- A weekly or biweekly conferring schedule with students.
- A way to organize the data collected through observation and conferring.
- Ongoing data review to flexibly group students for targeted strategy or skill work.

How can we know our students as readers? The *best* way to know readers is to *listen* to them read, *talk* to them about what they read, and take anecdotal notes or collect *data* about who they are and where they are as a reader. We have to spend time listening to them read to know if they are choosing books that are accessible and understandable as well as being challenging and providing opportunities to practice skills and strategies while developing a rich vocabulary.

The following sections discuss four essential look-fors of independent reading and application and include reflective questions to guide discussion about it in your school.

Teacher is conferring one-on-one with reader, assessing development, and recording data. Conferring is the teacher's opportunity to know each student as a reader, to observe each student applying the skills and strategies taught, and to monitor each student's reading development. An essential aspect of conferring is recording data. These rich data fill in the blanks left by summative, formal assessment data. Such data are necessary for daily instructional decision making.

Reflective Questions:

Is the teacher actively taking notes and talking with the student? Does the teacher have a system for collecting and recording observations, anecdotal notes, and other data during the conferring session?

Students are reading self-selected books from a bag or bin and applying strategies learned. Assigning texts for independent reading or leveling the classroom library takes away student choice and does not support the development of self-selection. Research indicates that choice is essential to motivation. Leveling is only a part of the process in book selection; interest, purpose, and motivation are also crucial. Independent reading every day for 30 minutes is a nonnegotiable part of the literacy block. This is the time when students practice and apply all of the components of a teacher's instruction on their own. This is when self-direction and independence emerge and flourish.

Reflective Questions:

Do the students have a consistent process or protocol for choosing texts for their book bag/bin? Do students have a way to log/graph what they have read, journal, or respond to reading using sticky notes to support strategy practice?

Students are conferring with teacher for reading skills and/ or demonstrating learning target. This is when a teacher finds out whether teaching was effective. The goal of every reading lesson must be that students can demonstrate the learning target on their own. Students should be talking about their text selection, applying strategies taught in whole-group lessons, and demonstrating good comprehension/vocabulary/fluency development.

> **Reflective Questions:**
>
> Do the students understand their partnership in the conferring process? Do the students have ownership in the content and goal setting for conferring sessions?

Students are actively working at some other connected literacy enhancement activity. Independent reading every day for 30 minutes is a nonnegotiable part of the literacy block. After completing this essential part of the literacy block, students can engage in other literacy activities to support and extend their learning.

> **Reflective Questions:**
>
> Do the seatwork or center activities present authentic and engaging opportunities for students to develop their literacy skills? How many students are reading self-selected texts independently?

Student Interaction and Understanding

Literacy instruction is a partnership between the teacher and students, so it is important to connect with students to assess understanding. The teacher ensures that the learning targets or instructional goals are woven through the gradual release from whole group to small group to independent learning applications. When possible during a Literacy Classroom Visit, observers briefly speak with two to three students to determine how well they understand the learning targets or lesson goal and what they are supposed to know, learn, do, and show. It is important to determine whether students know what they are learning and why, as well as how well they can self-assess whether their work meets expectations and what to do if they need help.

What an Exemplary School's LCV Data Look Like

Classroom Environment and Culture

- All classrooms have space for whole- and small-group instruction and independent reading.
- Resources are available to support literacy engagement.
- All teachers are actively working with students during all aspects of instruction.
- All students are engaged in various reading, writing, listening, speaking, and thinking activities.
- All classroom libraries contain a minimum of 300 books.
- Classroom libraries have a variety and balance of fiction and informational text across many reading levels.
- Books and resources are presented in displays and bins that support student self-selection.
- A self-selection strategy and book bin protocol are posted and used by students in all classrooms.
- Students have book bins or bags with several self-selected texts in them.
- All teachers have partnered with their students to create anchor charts or I-Charts that describe expectations for all aspects of instructional delivery.
- Students transition from whole group to small group to independent work knowing rituals, routines, and procedures.
- The walls of the classroom are "walls that teach."
- A variety of examples of student work that honor effort and accomplishments are displayed.
- Word walls are interactive, providing a visual scaffold that supports students' learning of sight words and/or vocabulary as they read and write.

Learning Target/Instructional Goal

- The learning target is clearly posted in the majority of classrooms.
- The majority of the learning targets identify performance criteria so that students understand what they are supposed to do and show as a result of instruction and practice.
- The teacher weaves the learning target through all aspects of instructional delivery.
- When asked, students can explain the learning target or what they are supposed to learn, do, and show.

Whole-Group Explicit Instruction

- Whole-group instruction is being conducted in approximately one-third of the classrooms visited (balancing instructional time among whole-group, small-group, and independent instructional experiences).
- The majority of teachers are explicitly teaching and modeling the performance criteria while thinking aloud about the thought processes and meaning making that skilled readers employ while reading.
- The vast majority of students in every classroom appear to be listening and are responding to the teacher and peers to support their learning.
- When teachers provide directions, students respond promptly and are able to follow through.
- Although much of the interaction is between teacher and students, student-to-student interactions are also observed in many classrooms.

Continued

What an Exemplary School's LCV Data Look Like (continued)

Small-Group Guided Practice

- The majority of teachers are coaching and supporting small groups of students reading texts.
- In classrooms where students are silently reading in small groups, the teacher is listening to each student read and is actively taking notes about students' progress.
- After the reading, the teacher prompts deep discussions about the text using higher-order questioning.
- In some classrooms, student-led discussions are taking place; students follow a framework or protocol to guide their discussions.
- In classrooms where students are leading their own small-group discussions, the teacher is actively observing and taking notes as students discuss texts.
- In many classrooms, students work together in pairs as they discuss their texts.
- Students are applying strategies taught in whole group with their peers in small groups.

Independent Reading and Application

- Most teachers who are not instructing whole group or meeting in small groups are actively conferring with individual students.
- Teachers record data as they confer with students.
- While conferring with students, teachers check students' fluency, comprehension, motivation and interest, goal setting, and strategy application.
- All students have bags or bins or some method of keeping self-selected texts in a tool kit to be used for independent reading and conferring.
- In many classrooms, students take the lead in their conferences, demonstrating their learning and application of strategies.
- Students in many classrooms write in their response journals or write on sticky notes and place them in their books.
- Students are able to answer the teachers' questions; many students elaborate when questioned about the text they are reading.
- Most students are either writing or reading independently; very little work other than authentic reading or writing is observed.

Student Interaction and Understanding

- When asked, students can clearly explain what they are learning.
- When asked, students can clearly explain what they need to do and show to demonstrate their learning.
- Students refer to the posted learning target while explaining their learning and the performance criteria.
- Students are observed practicing the learning target in small groups and on their own.

Additional Literacy Classroom Visit Forms

Literacy Classroom Visit Whole-School Instrument

Balanced Literacy Component of the Literacy Classroom Visit	KA	KB	KC	1A	1B	1C	2A	2B	2C	3A	3B	3C	4A	4B	4C	5A	5B	5C
Classroom Environment and Culture																		
Classroom structure and practices support a developing culture of literacy.																		
Students are actively and purposefully engaged in literacy-focused learning activities.																		
Classroom library is organized to support self-selection and class size/level (300+ texts).																		
Classroom library has a balance of fiction/informational texts at varied levels.																		
Rituals, routines, and procedures are in place (I-Charts, process for book selection, etc.).																		
Displays of student work show development and celebrate literacy learning.																		
Interactive word walls are used to support writing and vocabulary development.																		
Learning Target/Instructional Goal																		
Learning target/goal is posted in student-friendly language.																		
Learning target/goal identifies demonstration of learning (performance criteria).																		
Learning target/goal is taught and monitored across the gradual release of responsibility.																		
Observed Method of Instructional Delivery																		
Whole-group lesson or mini-lesson																		
Small-group lesson																		
Independent reading and application																		

Whole-Group Explicit Instruction

Teacher is leading a focused mini-lesson or lesson using time effectively for age range.														
Teacher is explicitly teaching/modeling effective skill/strategy (learning target).														
Students are actively listening, purposefully engaged, and interacting with teacher.														
Students are actively listening, purposefully engaged, and interacting with peers.														

Small-Group Guided Practice

Teacher is guiding students' reading, strategy application, and collaborative discussions.														
Teacher is listening to students read individually while others read quietly.														
Teacher is assessing strengths/needs and collecting anecdotal notes.														
Students are reading and discussing texts at their instructional level.														
Students are practicing the skill or strategy explicitly taught and modeled in whole group.														

Independent Reading and Application

Teacher is conferring one-on-one with reader.														
Teacher is assessing development and recording data.														
Students are reading self-selected books from a bag or bin and applying strategies.														
Students are conferring with teacher using skills and demonstrating learning target.														
Students are actively working at some other connected literacy enhancement activity.														

Continued

Literacy Classroom Visit Whole-School Instrument (continued)

Balanced Literacy Component of the Literacy Classroom Visit	KA	KB	KC	1A	1B	1C	2A	2B	2C	3A	3B	3C	4A	4B	4C	5A	5B	5C
Student Interaction and Understanding																		
Students can explain the skill/strategy.																		
Students know what they are supposed to learn and how they are expected to demonstrate that learning in whole or small group or on their own.																		
N/A (Did not speak with student).																		

Source: © 2015 by Bonnie D. Houck, EdD, and Sandi Novak. Used with permission.

Literacy Classroom Visit Data Analysis Framework Instrument

FOCUS: What is the focus area of this series of classroom visits?

CLASSROOM ENVIRONMENT AND CULTURE

1. **OBSERVATIONS:** Note observations from each identified component on the form.
2. **STRENGTHS:** List 1–2 strengths in the Classroom Environment and Culture section of the classroom visit data.
3. **NEEDS:** List 1–2 needs in the Classroom Environment and Culture section of the classroom visit data.

LEARNING TARGET/INSTRUCTIONAL GOAL

1. **OBSERVATIONS:** Note observations from each identified component on the form.
2. **STRENGTHS:** List 1–2 strengths in the Learning Target/Instructional Goal section of the classroom visit data.
3. **NEEDS:** List 1–2 needs in the Learning Target/Instructional Goal section of the classroom visit data.

OBSERVED METHOD OF INSTRUCTIONAL DELIVERY

1. **OBSERVATIONS:** Note observations from each identified component on the form.
2. **PATTERN:** Are the methods of instructional delivery balanced across the school, or is there an area of dominance?

WHOLE-GROUP EXPLICIT INSTRUCTION

1. **OBSERVATIONS:** Note observations from each identified component on the form.
2. **STRENGTHS:** List 1–2 strengths in the Whole-Group Explicit Instruction section of the classroom visit data.
3. **NEEDS:** List 1–2 needs in the Whole-Group Explicit Instruction section of the classroom visit data.

SMALL-GROUP GUIDED PRACTICE

1. **OBSERVATIONS:** Note observations from each identified component on the form.
2. **STRENGTHS:** List 1–2 strengths in the Small-Group Guided Practice section of the classroom visit data.
3. **NEEDS:** List 1–2 needs in the Small-Group Guided Practice section of the classroom visit data.

INDEPENDENT READING AND APPLICATION

1. **OBSERVATIONS:** Note observations from each identified component on the form.
2. **STRENGTHS:** List 1–2 strengths in the Independent Reading and Application section of the classroom visit data.
3. **NEEDS:** List 1–2 needs in the Independent Reading and Application section of the classroom visit data.

Continued

Literacy Classroom Visit Data
Analysis Framework Instrument *(continued)*

Summary Statements	
Strengths: List 3–4 overall strengths to share with staff.	**Needs:** List 1–2 high-priority needs to share with staff.

Professional Development
Possible professional learning to address needs:

APPENDIX C:
List of Videos

This section includes a list of the videos referenced in this book. The videos can be accessed at www.ascd.org/Publications/Books/Literacy-Unleashed-Book-Video-Clips.aspx.

Video 1.1. A district team gathers together to conduct LCVs in one elementary school.

Video 2.1. A 4th grade teacher demonstrates the gradual release of responsibility by modeling the learning target in whole group and then monitoring its application in small group and independent reading.

Video 3.1. A 4th grade teacher delivers a whole-group lesson on making an inference about a character.

Video 3.2. Small-group guided reading work connects to the whole-group lesson featured in Video 3.1.

Video 3.3. During independent reading, the 4th grade teacher assesses the application of the learning target modeled in Video 3.1 by conferring with individual students.

Video 4.1. A principal and literacy coach share the LCV process at a staff meeting.

Video 4.2. Five principals from one school district talk about how they informed their staff about the LCV Model and describe their teachers' reactions.

Video 4.3. An LCV team receives orientation during a meeting at Jonathan Elementary School with Joan MacDonald, a guest principal, serving as the facilitator.

Video 4.4. The Mounds View LCV team conducts its first classroom visit and then meets to calibrate the instrument.

Video 4.5. The Mounds View team discusses strengths and needs identified in their LCVs.

Video 4.6. Principals attending a four-day training sponsored by the Minnesota Elementary School Principals Association (MESPA) share their summary statements after school teams had conducted LCVs in each of their schools.

Video 5.1. Principals at MESPA talk about whole-group instruction as an identified area of need.

Video 5.2. A team from Gaithersburg Elementary School in Maryland meets to conduct LCVs, with a particular focus on independent reading.

Video 6.1. Principals at MESPA ponder where to begin when multiple areas of need have been identified.

Video 8.1. On day four of the four-day MESPA training, principals are trained in the LCV process.

Video 8.2. Mounds View principals talk about the value of using the LCV Model in the whole district.

References

Adams, M. J. (1990). *Beginning to read: Thinking and learning about print*. Cambridge, MA: Massachusetts Institute of Technology.

Allington, R. L. (2002). What I've learned about effective reading instruction from a decade of studying exemplary elementary classroom teachers. *Phi Delta Kappan, 83*(10), 740–747.

Anderson, M. (2011). Classroom displays: Keep the focus on student work. *ASCD Express, 6*(13). Retrieved from http://www.ascd.org/ascd-express/vol6/613-anderson.aspx?

Baker, L. (2002). Metacognition in comprehension instruction. In C. C. Block & M. Pressley (Eds.), *Comprehension instruction: Research-based best practices* (pp. 77–79). New York: Guilford Press.

Banilower, E. (2002). *Results of the 2001–2002 study of the impact of local systemic change initiative on student achievement in science*. Arlington, VA: National Science Foundation.

Batt, E. G. (2010). Cognitive coaching: A critical phase in professional development to implement sheltered instruction. *Teaching and Teacher Education, 26*, 997–1005.

Bear, D. R., Invernizzi, M., Templeton, S., & Johnston, F. (2000). *Words their way: Word study for phonics, vocabulary, and spelling*. Upper Saddle River, NJ: Prentice-Hall.

Blumenfeld, P. C., Kempler, T. M., Krajcik, J. S., & Blumenfeld, P. (2006). Motivation and cognitive engagement in learning environments. In R. K. Sawyer (Ed.), *Cambridge handbook of the learning sciences*. New York: Cambridge University Press.

Boehm, E., Dillon, D., Helman, L., Houck, B., Jordan, G., Peterson, D., et al. (2012). *The Balanced Literacy Gradual Release Model of Reading Instruction*.

Booth, D., & Rowsell, J. (2007). *The literacy principal: Leading, supporting and assessing reading and writing initiatives*. Ontario, Canada: Pembroke.

Bransford, J. D., Brown, A. L., & Cocking, R. R. (Eds.). (2000). *How people learn: Brain, mind, experience, and school*. Washington, DC: National Academy Press.

Bruner, J. (1960). *The process of education*. Cambridge, MA: Harvard University Press.

Bush, R. N. (1984). *Effective staff development in making schools more effective: Proceedings of three state conferences*. San Francisco: Far West Laboratory.

Byrnes, J. P. (2000). Using instructional time effectively. In L. Baker, M. J. Dreher, & J. T. Guthrie (Eds.), *Engaging young readers: Promoting achievement and motivation* (pp. 188–208). New York: Guilford Press.

Cantrell, S., Burns, L., & Callaway, P. (2009). Middle and high school content area teachers' perceptions about literacy teaching and learning. *Literacy Research and Instruction, 48*(1), 76–94.

Carnine, L., & Carnine, D. (2004).The interaction of reading skills and science content knowledge when teaching struggling secondary students. *Reading & Writing Quarterly, 20*, 203–218.

Cervone, L., & Martinez-Miller, P. (2007). Classroom walkthroughs as a catalyst for school improvement. *Leadership Compass, 4*(4). Retrieved from http://www.naesp.org/resources/2/Leadership_Compass/2007/LC2007v4n4a2.pdf

City, E., Elmore, R., Fiarman, S., & Teitel, L. (2009). *Instructional rounds in education: A network approach to improving teaching.* Cambridge, MA: Harvard Education Press.

Cole, P. (2005). *Leadership and professional learning: Forty actions leaders can take to improve professional learning.* (Seminar Series No. 150). Melbourne, Australia: Centre for Strategic Education. Retrieved from http://www.ptrconsulting.com.au/sites/default/files/Peter_Cole-Leadership_and_Professional_Learning.pdf

Cole, P. (2012). *Linking effective professional learning with effective teaching practice.* Melbourne, Australia: Australian Institute for Teaching and School Leadership. Retrieved from http://aitsl.edu.au/docs/default-source/professional-growth-resources/Research/linking_effective_professional_learning_with_effective_teaching_practice_cole_nov_2012.pdf?sfvrsn=2

Colvin, R., & Johnson, J. (2007). Know the game and cover the action. *Education Week, 27*(19), 36.

Croft, A., Coggshall, J., Dolan, M., Powers, E., & Killion, J. (2010). *Job-embedded professional development: What it is, who is responsible, and how to get it done well* [Issue brief]. Washington, DC: National Comprehensive Center for Teacher Quality. Retrieved from http://www.gtlcenter.org/sites/default/files/docs/JEPD%20Issue%20Brief.pdf

Darling-Hammond, L., & Bransford, J. (Eds.). (2005). *Preparing teachers for a changing world.* San Francisco: Jossey-Bass.

Darling-Hammond, L., Chung Wei, R., Andree, A., & Richardson, N. (2009). *Professional learning in the learning profession: A status report on teacher development in the United States and abroad.* Oxford, OH: National Staff Development Council.

DuFour, R., & Marzano, R. (2009). High-leverage strategies for principal leadership. *Educational Leadership, 66*(5), 62–68.

DuFour, R., & Mattos, M. (2013). How do principals really improve schools? *Educational Leadership, 70*(7), 34–40.

Duke, N. K., & Pearson, P. D. (2002). Effective practices for developing reading comprehension. In A. E. Farstrup & S. J. Samuels (Eds.), *What research has to say about reading instruction* (3rd ed., pp. 205–242). Newark, DE: International Reading Association.

Durkin, D. (1978). What classroom observations reveal about reading comprehension instruction. *Reading Research Quarterly, 14*, 481–533.

Ebert, E., Ebert, C., & Bentley, M. (2013). *The educator's field guide from organization to assessment (and everything in between).* Thousand Oaks, CA: Corwin. Retrieved from http://www.education.com/reference/article/curriculum-definition/

Ermeling, B. (2010). Tracing the effects of teacher inquiry on classroom practice. *Teaching and Teacher Education, 26*(3), 377–388.

Evers, T. (2011). *Common Core State Standards for literacy in all subjects.* Wisconsin Department of Public Instruction. Retrieved from https://dpi.wi.gov/sites/default/files/imce/cal/pdf/las-stds.pdf

Fink, E., & Resnick, L. B. (2001). Developing principals as instructional leaders. *Phi Delta Kappan, 82*(8), 598–606.

Fisher, C. W., & Adler, M. A. (1999). *Early reading programs in high poverty, high performing schools: A preliminary cross case analysis.* Paper presented at the annual meeting of the National Reading Conference, Orlando, Florida.

Fisher, D., & Frey, N. (2007). Implementing a schoolwide literacy framework: Improving achievement in an urban elementary school. *The Reading Teacher, 61*(1), 32–43.

Fredericks, J. A., Blumenfeld, P. C., & Paris, A. (2004). School engagement: Potential of the concept, state of the evidence. *Review of Educational Research, 74*(1), 59–109.

Fullan, M. (2001). *Whole school reform: Problems and promises.* Ontario Institute for Studies in Education, University of Toronto, Ontario, Canada. Retrieved from http://www.michaelfullan.ca/media/13396044810.pdf

Gallagher, K. (2003). *Reading reasons: Motivational mini-lessons for middle and high school.* Portland, ME: Stenhouse Publishers.

Ginsberg, M. (2001). By the numbers. *Journal of Staff Development, 22*(2), 44–47.

Ginsberg, M., & Murphy, D. (2002). How walkthroughs open doors. *Educational Leadership, 59*(8), 34–36.

Goodwin, B., & Miller, K. (2012). Research says good feedback is targeted, specific, timely. *Educational Leadership, 70*(1), 81–83.

Graham, S., & Hebert, M. A. (2010). *Writing to read: Evidence for how writing can improve reading* [A Carnegie Corporation Time to Act report]. Washington, DC: Alliance for Excellent Education.

Greenleaf, C., & Hinchman, K. (2009). Reimagining our inexperienced adolescent readers: From struggling, striving, marginalized, and reluctant to thriving. *Journal of Adolescent & Adult Literacy, 53*(1), 4–13.

Gulamhussein, A. (2013). *Teaching the teachers: Effective professional development in an era of high stakes accountability.* Alexandria, VA: Center for Public Education.

Guskey, T. (2014). Planning professional learning. *Educational Leadership, 71*(8), 10–16.

Hattie, J. (2008). *Visible learning: A synthesis of meta-analyses relating to achievement.* London: Routledge.

Heller, R., & Greenleaf, C. (2007). *Literacy instruction in the content areas: Getting to the core of middle and high school improvement.* Washington, DC: Alliance for Excellent Education.

Herman, R., Dawson, P., Dee, T., Greene, J., Maynard, R., Redding, S., et al. (2008). *Turning around chronically low-performing schools: A practice guide.* (NCEE #2008-4020). Washington, DC: National Center for Education Evaluation and Regional Assistance, Institute of Education Sciences, U.S. Department of Education. Retrieved from http://ies.ed.gov/ncee/wwc/pdf/practice_guides/Turnaround_pg_04181.pdf

Hoewing, B. L. (2011). *Orientations of literacy leadership among elementary school principals: Demographic and background trends* (Unpublished doctoral dissertation). University of Iowa. Retrieved from http://ir.uiowa.edu/etd/983

Hollie, S. (2011). *Culturally and linguistically responsive teaching and learning: Classroom practices for student success.* Huntington Beach, CA: Shell Education.

Hopkins, G. (2008). Walk-throughs are on the move. *Education World.* Retrieved from http://www.educationworld.com/a_admin/admin/admin405.shtml

Houck, B., & Boehm, E. (2014). *Professional learning model for teacher personalized learning.* Unpublished manuscript.

Houck, B., & Ross, K. (2012). Dismantling the myth of learning to read and reading to learn. *ASCD Express, 7*(11). Retrieved from http://www.ascd.org/ascd-express/vol7/711-houck.aspx

International Reading Association. (2000). *Providing books and other print materials for classroom and school libraries: A position statement of the International Reading Association.* Newark, DE: Author. Retrieved from http://www.literacyworldwide.org/docs/default-source/where-we-stand/providing-books-position-statement.pdf?sfvrsn=6

Irvin, J., Meltzer, J., Dean, N., & Mickler, M. J. (2010). *Taking the lead on adolescent literacy: Action steps for schoolwide success.* Thousand Oaks, CA: Corwin.

Jensen, E. (2005). *Teaching with the brain in mind* (2nd ed.). Alexandria, VA: ASCD.

Joftus, S. (2002). *Every child a graduate: A framework for an excellent education for all middle and high school students.* Washington, DC: Alliance for Excellent Education.

Johnson, D., & Foertsch, M. (2000). *Critical issue: Monitoring the school literacy program.* Naperville, IL: North Central Regional Educational Laboratory, Office of Educational Research and Improvement. Retrieved from http://files.eric.ed.gov /fulltext/ED480226.pdf

Joyce, B., & Showers, B. (1982). The coaching of teaching. *Educational Leadership, 40*(1), 4–10.

Juel, C. (1994). *Learning to read and write in one elementary school.* New York: Springer Verlag.

Knight, J. (2007). *Instructional coaching: A partnership approach to improving instruction.* Thousand Oaks, CA: Corwin.

Knight, J., & Cornett, J. (2009). *Studying the impact of instructional coaching.* Lawrence, KS: Kansas Coaching Project for the Center on Research on Learning.

Kosanovich, M. L., Reed, D. K., & Miller, D. H. (2010). *Bringing literacy strategies into content instruction: Professional learning for secondary-level teachers.* Portsmouth, NH: RMC Research Corporation, Center on Instruction.

Krashen, S. (2004). *The power of reading: Insights from the research* (2nd ed.). Portsmouth, NH: Heinemann & Westview, CT: Libraries Unlimited.

Learning Forward. (2011). *Standards for professional learning* (4th ed.). Oxford, OH: Author. Retrieved from http://learningforward.org/standards-for-professional-learning#.Vf3J0t9VhBc

Leithwood, K. (2002). *Organizational learning and school improvement.* Greenwich, CT: JAI.

Leithwood, K., & Seashore-Louis, K. (2011). *Linking leadership to student learning.* San Francisco: Jossey-Bass.

Lesley, M. (2004). Looking for critical literacy with postbaccalaureate content area literacy students. *Journal of Adolescent & Adult Literacy, 48*(4), 320–334.

Liu, V., & Mulfinger, L. (2011). Making it meaningful: Building a fair evaluation system. *TE2 Community Brief,* 1–8.

Margolis, J. (2008). When teachers face teachers: Listening to the resource "right down the hall." *Teaching Education, 19*(4), 293–310.

Marzano, R. (2003). *What works in schools: Translating research into action.* Alexandria, VA: ASCD.

Marzano, R., Pickering, D., & Pollock, J. (2004). *Classroom instruction that works: Research-based strategies for increasing student achievement* (2nd ed.). Alexandria, VA: ASCD.

Means, B., Toyama, Y., Murphy, R., Bakia, M., & Jones, K. (2010). *Evaluation of evidence-based practices in online learning: A meta-analysis and review of online learning studies.* Washington, DC: U.S. Department of Education, Office of Planning, Evaluation, and Policy Development, Policy and Program Studies Service. Retrieved from https://www2.ed.gov/rschstat/eval/tech/evidence-based-practices/finalreport.pdf

Mehta, J., Hess, F., & Schwartz, R. (2011, March 28). The futures of school reform: An introduction and an invitation. *Education Week, 30*(26). Retrieved from http://www.edweek.org/ew/collections/futures-of-school-reform/invitation.html

MET Project. (2013). *Feedback for better teaching: Nine principles for using measures of effective teaching* [Measures of Effective Teaching Project white paper]. Seattle, WA: Bill & Melinda Gates Foundation. Retrieved from http://k12education .gatesfoundation.org/wp-content/uploads/2015/05/MET_Feedback-for-Better-Teaching_Principles-Paper.pdf

Miller, D., & Moss, B. (2013). *No more independent reading without support.* Portsmouth, NH: Heinemann.

Mizell, H. (2009). Top performance requires that system leaders develop principals' learning. *The Learning System.* Oxford, OH: National Staff Development Council. Retrieved from http://learningforward.org/docs/learning-system/sys2-09mizell .pdf?sfvrsn=2

Mizell, H. (2010). *Why professional development matters.* Oxford, OH: Learning Forward.

Morrow, L. M., Reutzel, D. R., & Casey, H. (2006). Organization and management of exemplary language arts teaching: Classroom environments, grouping practices, and exemplary instruction. In C. Evertson & C. Weinstein (Eds.), *Handbook of classroom management* (pp. 559–581). Mahwah, NJ: Lawrence Erlbaum Associates.

Moss, B., & Young, T. (2010). *Creating lifelong readers through independent reading.* Newark, DE: International Reading Association.

Moss, C., & Brookhart, S. (2015). *Formative classroom walkthroughs: How principals and teachers collaborate to raise student achievement.* Alexandria, VA: ASCD.

Moss, C., Brookhart, S., & Long, B. (2011). Knowing your learning target. *Educational Leadership, 68*(6), 66–69.

National Assessment of Educational Progress. (2014). *The nation's report card.* Washington, DC: Author. Retrieved from http://www.nationsreportcard.gov /reading_math_2013/#/executive-summary

National Early Literacy Panel. (2008). *Developing early literacy: Report of the National Early Literacy Panel.* Washington, DC: National Institute for Literacy.

National Governors Association Center for Best Practices. (2005). *Building the foundation for bright futures: A governor's guide to school readiness.* Washington, DC: Author.

National Governors Association Center for Best Practices & the Council of Chief State School Officers. (2010). Common Core State Standards for English language arts & literacy in history/social studies, science, and technical subjects. Washington, DC: Author.

National Institute of Child Health and Human Development. (2000). *Teaching children to read: An evidence-based assessment of the scientific research literature on reading and its implications for reading instruction* [Report of the National Reading Panel]. (NIH Publication No. 00-4769). Washington, DC: Author.

Newingham, B. (2015). Give your classroom library a boost. *Scholastic, Inc.* Retrieved from http://www.scholastic.com/teachers/article/give-your-classroom-library-boost

Novak, S. (2014). *Student-led discussions: How do I promote rich conversations about books, videos, and other media?* Alexandria, VA: ASCD.

Pearson, P. D., & Gallagher, M. C. (1983). The instruction of reading comprehension. *Contemporary Educational Psychology, 8,* 317–344.

Pinnell, G. S., Fountas, I. C., & Giacobbe, M. E. (1998). *Word matters: Teaching phonics and spelling in the reading/writing classroom.* Portsmouth, NH: Heinemann.

Pitler, H., with Goodwin, B. (2008, Summer). Classroom walkthroughs: Learning to see the trees *and* the forest. *Changing Schools, 58,* 9–11. Retrieved from http://www .mikemcmahon.info/ClassroomObservation.pdf

Pressley, M., & Allington, R. (2014). *Reading instruction that works: The case for balanced teaching* (4th ed.). New York: Guilford Press.

Protheroe, N. (2009). Using classroom walkthroughs to improve instruction. *Principal, 88*(4), 30–34.

Reeves, D. (2008). *Reframing teacher leadership to improve your school.* Alexandria, VA: ASCD.

Reeves, D. (2010). *Transforming professional development into student results.* Alexandria, VA: ASCD.

Reutzel, D. R., Jones, C. D., & Newman, T. (2010). Scaffolded silent reading. In E. H. Hiebert & D. R. Reutzel (Eds.), *Revisiting silent reading: New directions for teachers and researchers* (pp. 129–150). Newark, DE: International Reading Association.

Reutzel, D. R., & Morrow, L. M. (2007). Promoting and assessing effective literacy learning classroom environments. In R. McCormick & J. Paratore (Eds.), *Classroom literacy assessment: Making sense of what students know and do* (pp. 33–49). New York: Guilford Press.

Reynolds, D., & Teddlie, C. (2000). The process of school effectiveness. In C. Teddlie & D. Reynolds (Eds.), *The international handbook of school effectiveness research* (pp. 134–159). New York: Routledge.

Rock, T. C., & Levin, B. B. (2002). Collaborative action research projects: Enhancing preservice teacher development in professional development schools. *Teacher Education Quarterly, 29*, 7–21.

Schmoker, M. (2006). *Results now: How we can achieve unprecedented improvements in teaching and learning.* Alexandria, VA: ASCD.

Schooling, P., Toth, M., & Marzano, R. (2013). *The critical importance of a common language of instruction.* West Palm Beach, FL: Learning Sciences Marzano Center & Learning Sciences International. Retrieved from http://www.marzanocenter.com /files/Common%20Language%20of%20Instruction%5B1%5D.pdf

Schwartzbeck, T. D. (2002). *Choosing a model and types of models: How to find what works for your school* [Research brief]. Washington, DC: National Clearinghouse for Comprehensive School Reform.

Scott, M. (2012). *The role of dialogue and inquiry in district implementation of classroom walkthroughs at four elementary schools* (Doctoral dissertation). Retrieved from ProQuest Dissertations & Theses. (UMI No. 3524040.)

Showers, B. (1984). *Peer coaching: A strategy for facilitating transfer of training.* Eugene, OR: Centre for Educational Policy and Management.

Skretta, J. (2008). *Walkthroughs: A descriptive study of Nebraska high school principals' use of walkthrough teacher observation process* (Doctoral dissertation). Available from ProQuest Dissertations & Theses (UMI No. 3297740.)

Slinger, J. L. (2004). Cognitive coaching: Impact on students and influence on teachers. *Dissertation Abstracts International, 65*(7), 2567. (University Microfilms No. 3138974.)

Snow, C. E., Griffin, P., & Burns, M. S. (Eds.). (2005). *Knowledge to support the teaching of reading: Preparing teachers for a changing world.* San Francisco: Jossey-Bass.

Spillane, J. P. (2006). *Distributed leadership.* San Francisco: Jossey-Bass.

Stein, M. K., & Nelson, B. S. (2003). Leadership content knowledge. *Educational Evaluation and Policy Analysis, 25*(4), 423–448.

Stephens, D., Morgan, D., Donnelly, A., DeFord, D., Young, J., & Seaman, M. (2007). *The South Carolina Reading Initiative: NCTE's Reading Initiative as a statewide staff development project.* Urbana, IL: National Council of Teachers of English. Retrieved from http://www.ncte.org/library/NCTEFiles/Resources/Magazine /SCRI_Report.pdf

Stout, J. A., Kachur, D. S., & Edwards, C. L. (2009). *Classroom walkthroughs to improve teaching and learning.* New York: Routledge.

Strickland, D. (2015). Balanced literacy: Practical strategies to help you build a truly balanced classroom literacy program. *Instructor Online Magazine.* Scholastic, Inc. Retrieved from http://www.scholastic.com/teachers/article/balanced-literacy

Sturtevant, E. G. (2003). *The literacy coach: A key to improving teaching and learning in secondary schools.* Washington DC: Alliance for Excellent Education.

Taylor, B. (2007). *The what and the how of good classroom reading instruction in the elementary grades.* Minneapolis, MN: University of Minnesota Center for Reading Research. Retrieved from http://www.cehd.umn.edu/reading/documents/reports /taylor-report.pdf

Taylor, B. M., Pressley, M., & Pearson, P. D. (2002). Research-supported characteristics of teachers and schools that promote reading achievement. In B. M. Taylor & P. D. Pearson (Eds.), *Teaching reading: Effective schools, accomplished teachers* (pp. 361–374). Mahwah, NJ: Erlbaum.

Tomlinson, C. A. (2014). *The differentiated classroom: Responding to the needs of all learners* (2nd ed.). Alexandria, VA: ASCD.

Tomlinson, C. A., & Allan, S. D. (2000). *Leadership for differentiating schools and classrooms.* Alexandria, VA: ASCD.

Torres, M. (2006, March 27–31). *Literacy and lifelong learning: The linkages.* Paper presented at the ADEA 2006 Biennial Meeting, Libreville, Gabon.

Truesdale, W. T. (2003). The implementation of peer coaching on the transferability of staff development to classroom practice in two selected Chicago public elementary schools. *Dissertation Abstracts International, 64*(11), 3923. (University Microfilms No. 3112185.)

Tyson, K. (2012). How does your classroom library grow? Top tips to create an effective classroom library. *Learning Unlimited.*

UNESCO. (2011). *Creating and sustaining literate environments.* Bangkok, Thailand: Author. Retrieved from http://unesdoc.unesco.org/images/0021/002146/214653E .pdf

Vacca, R. T., Vacca, J. L., & Mraz, M. (2013). *Content area reading: Literacy and learning across the curriculum* (11th ed.). Upper Saddle River, NJ: Pearson.

Wade, S. E., & Moje, E. B. (2000). The role of text in classroom learning. In M. Kamil, P. Mosenthal, R. Barr, & P. D. Pearson (Eds.), *The handbook of research on reading* (Volume III, pp. 609–627). Mahwah, NJ: Erlbaum.

Wei, R. C., Darling-Hammond, L., & Adamson, F. (2010). *Professional development in the United States: Trends and challenges.* Dallas, TX: National Staff Development Council.

Wolfersberger, M., Reutzel, D. R., Sudweeks, R., & Fawson, P. F. (2004). Developing and validating the Classroom Literacy Environmental Profile (CLEP): A tool for examining the "print richness" of elementary classrooms. *Journal of Literacy Research, 36*(2), 211–272.

Yoon, K. S., Duncan, T., Lee, S. W., Scarloss, B., & Shapley, K. L. (2007). *Reviewing the evidence on how teacher professional development affects student achievement.* (Issues and Answers Report, REL 2007–No. 033). Washington, DC: U.S. Department of Education, Institute of Education Sciences.

Zepeda, S. J. (2007). *Instructional supervision: Applying tools and concepts.* Larchmont, NY: Eye on Education.

Index

Page numbers followed by an italicized *f* or *t* indicate information contained in figures or tables, respectively.

anthology series readers, 28
assessment, student self-, 39
audiobooks, 25
authentic learning, 25
Autumn Ridge Elementary School
    about, 50–51
    LCV data, 54
    next steps and progress, 57–58
    summary statements, 56

Balanced Literacy Gradual Release
    Model of Reading Instruction
    about, 21, 22*f*–23*f*, 39–40, 45
    professional development for,
        81–82, 88–92
balanced literacy instruction, 12,
    19–20, 21, 28, 115
Barnum Elementary School (MN),
    7–8
basal series readers, 28
Bel Air Elementary School (New
    Brighton, MN), 111–112
Bluff Creek Elementary School
    (Chanhassen, MN), 41–42
Booth, David, 9

classroom environment and culture
    inconsistent data across school,
        61–65, 62*f*, 64*f*
    LCV look-fors, 14*f*, 21–26, 24*f*,
        126–129
    LVCC look-fors, 99–100, 99*f*
    teacher survey instrument, 31*f*

classroom libraries, 25, 44, 62, 63–65,
    64*f*
Classroom Library Checklist, 44, 64*f*
classroom visits, traditional model of,
    10–12
Clearview Elementary School, 82–88
coaching school leaders, 119
college preparedness, 2
Common Core State Standards, 2, 3
comprehension development, 19
conferences. *See* reading conferences
Content Classroom Instrument,
    (LVCC), 96*f*–97*f*, 98–104, 99*f*, 101*f*,
    102*f*, 103*f*, 104*f*
content classrooms, involvement of.
    See whole-school involvement
culture of literacy, 12, 18, 24*f*, 81,
    119–120, 123, 126. *See also* classroom
    environment and culture
curriculum, 28

Daily5/CAFE Model, 28
data analysis, LCV
    about, 59–60
    classroom environment and
        culture inconsistent, 61–65,
        62*f*, 64*f*
    common patterns and solutions,
        60–75
    Data Analysis Framework
        Instrument, 145–146
    independent reading and appli-
        cation problems, 72–74, 73*f*,
        74*f*–75*f*

data analysis, LCV (*continued*)
    initial pattern identification, 53
    learning targets not guiding
      instruction, 65–67, 66*f*
    of small-group guided practice,
      69–72, 70*f*, 71*f*, 72*f*
    and summary statements, 55
    whole-group instruction not
      effective, 67–69, 68*f*, 69*f*
Data Analysis Framework Instru-
    ment, 53, 62
data collection, LCV
    implementation concerns, 46–47,
      48, 49, 51
    importance of, 10
    teacher survey on, 32*f*
Davis, Julie, 33
differentiated instruction, 13, 19
"Discussing the Components of Liter-
    acy Classroom Visits," 45, 48
district-wide implementation
    culture of literacy and, 119–120
    district leaders' roles, 115–117, 119
    district role in school improve-
      ment, 113–114
    LCV role in supporting district
      plans, 114–115, 116*f*
    professional learning for princi-
      pals, 118–119
dropout rates, 2

e-books, 25
employment, literacy skills for, 2
engagement, student, 25, 34, 69

Fawcett, Janet, 30
fluency, 19
Foertsch, Mary, 29

Geis, Steven, 20, 44
gradual release of responsibility
    about, 12, 13, 20–21, 26, 28, 68,
      115
    professional development for,
      88–92
Gurbada, Phil, 49
Guskey, Thomas, 78

Hancock School District, 99–104

Herman, Rebecca, 43

implementation of Literacy Class-
    room Visit (LCV) model. *See also*
    data analysis; data collection; team
    training, LCV
    buy-in, 30, 45
    individualizing purpose, 44
    initial staff meeting, 45–46
    LCV instrument enhancements,
      61, 67, 74, 75–76
    LCV team, 47–50, 51–52
    ongoing practice, 17
    planning next steps and visits, 57
    planning staff discussion and
      communication, 54–55
    reflection and debriefing, 53
    staff preparation, 44
    staff survey, 46
    summary statements, 55–56
    visits format and process, 51–52
incarceration rates, 2
independent reading application and
    demonstration of learning
    in Balanced Literacy Gradual
      Release model, 22*f*–23*f*
    LCV instrument enhancements
      to target, 74
    LCV look-fors, 15*f*, 37–38, 38*f*,
      136–138
    LVCC look-fors, 103–104, 103*f*
    not enough time devoted to,
      72–74, 73*f*, 74*f*–75*f*
    professional development for,
      82–88
    and teacher survey instrument,
      32*f*
    whole-group work not effectively
      preparing students for, 67–69,
      68*f*, 69*f*
independent reading locations, 24
instructional goals. *See* learning tar-
    gets/instructional goals
instructional practices. *See also* inde-
    pendent reading application and
    demonstration of learning; learning
    targets/instructional goals; small-
    group guided practice; whole-group
    explicit instruction and modeling

instructional practices. *See also* independent reading application and demonstration of learning; learning targets/instructional goals; small-group guided practice; whole-group explicit instruction and modeling (*continued*)
  in balanced literacy approach, 19–20
  data collection and analysis of, 10, 32, 65–67, 66*f*
instructional rounds, 10–12
Instructional Supervision (Zepeda), 18

jobs outlook, 2
Johnson, Debra, 29

Learning Forward, 66, 83, 116–117
learning targets/instructional goals
  on LCV instrument, 33–34, 34*f*
  LCV instrument enhancements to address, 67
  LCV look-fors, 14*f*, 130
  LVCC (content areas) look-fors, 100–101, 101*f*
  not guiding instruction, 65–67, 66*f*
  professional development for, 81
  teacher survey instrument, 31*f*
libraries, classroom, 25, 44, 62, 63–65, 64*f*
Literacy Academy, 118
Literacy Classroom Visit (LCV) model
  about, 12–13, 123
  classroom library, 25
  classroom structure, 21–24, 24*f*
  data analysis (*See* data analysis, LCV)
  data collection (*See* data collection, LCV)
  development of, 3–4
  district-wide implementation (*See* district-wide implementation)
  exemplary data set for, 139–140
  implementation of (*See* implementation of Literacy Classroom Visit (LCV) model)

Literacy Classroom Visit (LCV) model (*continued*)
  instructional practice "look-fors," 13–15, 14*f*–15*f*
  LCV Content Classroom Instrument, 96*f*–97*f*
  LCV instrument, 14*f*–15*f*, 33–38, 34*f*, 35*f*, 36*f*, 38*f*, 45, 48
  LCV instrument enhancements, 61, 67, 74, 75–76
  LCV Whole-School Instrument, 46–47, 76, 142–144
  literacy-focused activities and student engagement, 25
  principals' literacy instruction knowledge and, 26–28
  process, 16
  professional learning (*See* professional learning)
  protocol for, 124–125
  purpose, 16
  recommendations, 7–8, 41–42, 111–112
  rituals and routines, 25–26
  role in supporting district improvement efforts, 114–115, 116*f*
  structure of classroom visits, 16–17
  summary of, 121–122
  Teacher Balanced Literacy Survey, 30, 31*f*–32*f*, 44, 46
  team training (*See* team training, LCV)
  tenets of, 19–21
  uses for leaders of, 13, 17
  video resources, 147–148
  walls and displays, 26
  whole-school involvement (*See* whole-school involvement)
"Literacy Classroom Visit Protocol," 49, 123–140
Literacy Classroom Visit Whole-School Instrument, 46–47, 76, 142–144
literacy education, 1–3, 10
The Literacy Principal (Booth and Rowsell), 9
literacy skills, in U.S., 2

Literacy Visit in the Content Classroom Instrument (LVCC), 96f–97f, 98–104, 99f, 101f, 102f, 103f, 104f

MacDonald, Joan, 41–42
McHenry Elementary School, 88–92
Means, Barbara, 59
Mizell, Hayes, 66

National Assessment of Educational Progress, 2
National Early Literacy Panel, 19, 89
National Reading Panel, 19, 89

oral language development, 19
Otterson, Pete, 118

peer engagement, 24
phonemic awareness, 19
principals, school
    building literacy leadership capacity, 9–10
    and classroom visits, 10–12
    debriefing LCV teams, 53
    designing professional learning, 79, 81–82
    group facilitation for, 119
    and implementation of LCV model, 43, 45, 47, 50–51
    literacy instruction knowledge, 26–28
    professional learning for, 118–119
    role of, 9, 10
    staff communication plans, 54–55
    whole-school buy-in and engagement, 95–98
professional development. See professional learning
professional learning
    about, 11, 78–79
    areas to target, 81–82, 86
    assessing and monitoring, 87–88, 92–93
    design for literacy, 79, 80f
    examples of effective, 82–92
    focus on balanced literacy and gradual release of responsibility, 88–92

professional learning (continued)
    focus on independent reading, 82–88
    independent application and coaching, 85–86
    PLC discussions, 84–85, 90–91
    professional readings, 84
    for school principals, 118–119
protocol, LCV, 49, 123–140
purposeful student engagement, 13

Reader's/Writer's Workshop Model, 28
reading conferences, 41, 72–73
reading instruction, 21
rituals and routines, classroom, 25–26, 65
Rowsell, Jennifer, 9

school improvement, district role in, 113–114
school-wide involvement. See whole-school involvement
science classroom, middle school, 105–107
small-group guided practice
    in Balanced Literacy Gradual Release model, 22f–23f
    coaching vs. teaching in, 69–72, 70f, 71f, 72f
    LCV look-fors, 14f, 36–37, 36f, 133–135
    LVCC look-fors, 102–103
    professional development for, 81, 91
    teacher survey instrument, 32f
small-group instruction, 24
social studies classroom, high school, 107–109
Standards for Professional Learning (Learning Forward), 83, 116–117
student interaction and understanding
    LCV look-fors, 15f, 39, 39f, 138
    LVCC look-fors, 104f
Student-Led Discussions: How do I promote Rich Conversations About Books, Videos, and Other Media (Novak), 37

student self-assessment, 39
student work, posted, 26, 61
summary statements, 55–56

Teacher Balanced Literacy Survey, 30,
    31*f*–32*f*, 44, 46
teachers. *See also* professional learn-
    ing; Teacher Balanced Literacy
    Survey
        buy-in, 30, 45
        and classroom visits, 10–12
        initial staff meeting on LCV,
            45–46
        planning discussion and commu-
            nication with, 54–55
        teacher-centered instruction, 71
        walkthroughs and evaluation, 12
        whole-school buy-in and engage-
            ment, 95–98
team training, LCV
        about, 47–48
        data collection protocols, 49
        document review, 48–49
        focus development, 48
        schedules of visits, 49–50
text, complexity of, 2
think-pair-shares, 35
trust, 15

vocabulary, 19

walkthroughs, 10–12
walls and displays, classroom, 26

welfare status, 2
whole-group explicit instruction and
    modeling
        in Balanced Literacy Gradual
            Release model, 22*f*–23*f*
        LCV look-fors, 14*f*, 34–36, 35*f*,
            131–133
        LVCC look-fors, 101–102, 102*f*
        not effectively preparing stu-
            dents for independent applica-
            tion, 67–69, 68*f*, 69*f*
        professional development for, 81,
            90–91
        teacher survey instrument, 31*f*
Whole-School Instrument, LCV,
    46–47, 76, 142–144
whole-school involvement
        about, 94–95
        high school social studies exam-
            ple, 107–109
        Literacy Visit in the Content
            Classroom (LVCC) instrument,
            96*f*–97*f*, 98–104, 99*f*, 101*f*, 102*f*,
            103*f*, 104f
        middle school science example,
            105–107
        teacher buy-in and engagement,
            95–98
Wiegand, Dawn, 111–112
word walls, 26, 63

Zepeda, Sally J., 18

About the Authors

Bonnie D. Houck, EdD, brings a lifelong passion for education and literacy to her work as a consultant, coach, speaker, and trainer who specializes in literacy leadership development and positive school change. She combines a wealth of leadership experiences ranging from school and district leadership to state-level administration. Bonnie is currently the coordinator of the K–12 Teacher of Reading Program at the University of Minnesota, provides training through the Minnesota Elementary School Principals' Association, and works with many schools and districts as a coach and consultant. Previously, Bonnie served as the state reading specialist for the Minnesota Department of Education and was the program director for the Education and Learning program at a leading philanthropic organization. These experiences, combined with more than 25 years of experience as a teacher, specialist, literacy coach, literacy coordinator, and university instructor, culminate in deep knowledge of the necessary elements of school reform and the field of literacy education. Bonnie can be reached at www.HouckEd.com or houckreadz@gmail.com.

Sandi Novak is an education consultant and author of the ASCD Arias *Student-Led Discussions: How Do I Promote Rich Conversations About Books, Videos, and Other Media?* She has more than 30 years of experience as an assistant superintendent, principal, curriculum and professional learning director, and teacher. Her current work in consulting is focused on leadership and improving students' reading. During the last four years, she has consulted with Scholastic Book Fairs as it partnered with schools to improve independent reading. Through this work, she has collaborated with schools across the United States to help enhance their schoolwide independent reading cultures using many of the processes, procedures, and resources described in this book. Specifically, she has led professional learning and coached leaders about the use of the Literacy Classroom Visit Model to guide professional learning and collaborative practices in their schools. She can be reached at www.snovakeducational services.com or snovak9133@aol.com.

Related Resources

At the time of publication, the following ASCD resources were available (ASCD stock numbers appear in parentheses). For up-to-date information about ASCD resources, go to www.ascd.org. You can search the complete archives of *Educational Leadership* at http://www.ascd.org/el.

ASCD EDge®
Exchange ideas and connect with other educators on the social networking site ASCD EDge at http://ascdedge.ascd.org.

Print Products
A Close Look at Close Reading: Teaching Students to Analyze Complex Texts, Grades 6–12 by Barbara Moss, Diane Lapp, Maria Grant, and Kelly Johnson (#115002)
Differentiated Literacy Coaching: Scaffolding for Student and Teacher Success by Mary Catherine Moran (#107053)
Effective Literacy Coaching: Building Expertise and a Culture of Literacy (An ASCD Action Tool) by Shari Frost, Roberta Buhle, and Camille Blachowicz (#109044)
Formative Classroom Walkthroughs: How Principals and Teachers Collaborate to Raise Student Achievement by Connie M. Moss and Susan M. Brookhart (#115003)
The Fundamentals of Literacy Coaching by Amy Sandvold and Maelou Baxter (#107084)
Read, Write, Lead: Breakthrough Strategies for Schoolwide Literacy Success by Regie Routman (#113016)
Teaching the Core Skills of Listening and Speaking by Erik Palmer (#114012)
Total Literacy Techniques: Tools to Help Students Analyze Literature and Informational Texts by Pérsida Himmele, William Himmele, and Keely Potter (#114009)

DVD
ASCD Master Class Leadership Series (Five DVDs) (#613026)
The Innovators: Integrating Literacy into Curriculum DVD (#613070)

ASCD PD Online® Courses
Building a Schoolwide Independent Reading Culture (#PD15OC006M)
Common Core Literacy Pack (#PDQKCCLP)

For more information: send e-mail to member@ascd.org; call 1-800-933-2723 or 703-578-9600, press 2; send a fax to 703-575-5400; or write to Information Services, ASCD, 1703 N. Beauregard St., Alexandria, VA 22311-1714 USA.

WHOLE CHILD
TENETS

1 **HEALTHY**
Each student enters school healthy and learns about and practices a healthy lifestyle.

2 **SAFE**
Each student learns in an environment that is physically and emotionally **safe** for students and adults.

3 **ENGAGED**
Each student is actively engaged in learning and is connected to the school and broader community.

4 **SUPPORTED**
Each student has access to personalized learning and is **supported** by qualified, caring adults.

5 **CHALLENGED**
Each student is challenged academically and prepared for success in college or further study and for employment and participation in a global environment.

THE WHOLE CHILD

ASCD's Whole Child approach is an effort to transition from a focus on narrowly defined academic achievement to one that promotes the long-term development and success of all children. Through this approach, ASCD supports educators, families, community members, and policymakers as they move from a vision about educating the whole child to sustainable, collaborative actions.

Literacy Unleashed: Fostering Excellent Reading Instruction Through Classroom Visits relates to the **challenged** tenet.

For more about the Whole Child approach, visit
www.wholechildeducation.org.

LEARN. TEACH. LEAD.